Yellow Orang-Utan Industries

Yellow Orang-Utan Industries
by Simon Gray

Manuscript produced 1997-2010
PDF edition, 2020, ISBN: 9780648867210
Paperback, print on demand edition, 2020, ISBN: 9780648867227

Cover image by Joel Catchlove, originally appeared on the cover of the
zine, **The Electric Ape Omnibus, Volume 2** published by The Wild Oat
Collective, 2004. Used with permission via a friendly email exchange.

Quotations heading each chapter are credited where Google-searching
could clarify, texts cited were respectively authored, in order of appearance
by: Louis Simpson; John Kenneth Galbraith; Amory Lovins, Hunter Louis
& Paul Hawken; The Motion Picture Association of America; Ken Kesey;
M.B.V Roberts; Jennifer Lynch; & David E. Kelley.

Typeset with Myriad Pro by Adobe & Hoefler Text by Apple.

Cataloguing-in-Publication data, via National Library of Australia:
Author: Gray, Simon.
Title: Yellow Orang-Utan Industries/ Simon Gray.
Best Dewey guess: 820

For Robyn

Yellow Orang-Utan Industries

Simon Gray

1.

There is something compelling about looking at scenes in which humans have failed.

At seven twenty-nine and fifteen seconds, the president of Yellow Orang-Utan Industries was going blind again. He'd flicked a switch. A loud blaring noise hammered the room and the Wall-span TV flickered together to form images. He could only discern a blur, and the sound hurt his ears. He'd need fresh eyes. That meant an annoying operation. The blurry picture and the noise was too much. He turned the TV off and crawled back into the inviting recesses of his bed. The static clung to him like a tick. It tickled him, created a pleasant feeling. He rubbed his weak eyes. He flicked away from his pillow a small mess of dead skin and hair. It made the pillow seem as good as new, a clean fresh pillow, excepting exhales of his stale breath. The time was seven thirty.

At nine thirty a woman walked into the room. Her name was Gertrude.

"Good morning sir." Gertrude said to the lump on the bed.

"Good morning Gertrude," the president of Yellow Orang-Utan Industries replied. The small man poked his head out of the sheets. He eyed Gertrude. She was physically perfect. He had made her that way. When he paid for her first implant, a long time ago, the new appearance was surprising and exciting. Although he still paid for all the other implants and operations, it seemed a little more awkward now. Today Gertrude wore a red dress, a blue jacket and carried a clip-board.

"What do you want to do today sir?"

The president paid Gertrude lots of money to work for him, a habitual day-in, day-out routine accompanying the president, administering help when needed. He'd paid for all the cosmetic surgery that had made her look so pretty, and very popular in the local clubs and bars. She looked at the weedy little man wrapped tightly in his artificial pouch, and hated him.

"What do you mean, what do I want to do today? I thought I had to negotiate the market hackers contracts today...But it also seems I need another eye operation." He thought about an attempt to look like he was trying to leave his bed, but decided against it.

"I'd like to get the operation done as soon as possible so I think I'll have that first as you seem to suggest I have a little range of free choice today. Call the doctor, will you?" A little bit of fear crept stealthily into his brain as he remembered what cleaning yourself in the morning entailed.

"Very well sir, shall you get up now while I go do that?" Gertrude asked. Her sweet voice echoed in the old man's head, encouragement enough to leave such a splendid warm cocoon, almost.

"I suppose so." The president of Yellow Orang-Utan Industries moaned. Gertrude walked out of the room and the president sat up quickly, weird dizzying sensations entered his head. He fell against a bed post, suddenly aware of the stiffness in his old bony limbs.

"Ouch," he mouthed to himself. Gertrude returned to the room.

"The appointment is at a quarter to eleven sir. It's good to see you standing," she said. The president could tell she was quietly laughing at his stiff form leaning semi-naked against the bed-post.

"Well don't just stand there, get me out of these Y-fronts and into something more comfortable!" he snapped.

"Yes sir." Gertrude stifled another laugh. The time was nine forty-one.

At eleven thirty the president of Yellow Orang-Utan Industries awoke with a start. Crisper images than the ones he remembered earlier that morning appeared in front of him. His eyes felt numb as if they'd been replaced with the organic equivalent of worn glass marbles, and their sockets like someone had shoved their fingers in them and had a good tug at his eyeballs. Somebody had.

"There you are, sir. Good morning. Wide awake now are we?" The familiar face of Dr. Westaway enquired. The president looked down at his body in the hospital bed and nodded.

"Good. The operation went off without a hitch. I've just given you a dose of painkillers that should last long enough for you not to feel any trouble in those eyes and a wakey shot. You're ready to go."

"Thank you doctor," the president said while he was wheeled away. Dr. Westaway waved back and grinned. Dr. Westaway had no idea that was the president of Yellow Orang-Utan Industries. To the doctor it was just another rich client, and an old one at that.

"Gertrude?"

"Yes sir?" Gertrude replied, later, in another room in the hospital.

"What colour are they?"

"Pardon?" Gertrude asked from the proximity of the president's waist as she began to button his shirt.

"My eyes, what colour are they?" The president repeated. Gertrude glanced up to look at his face. The smell of the hospital and the president's familiar body odour wafted around her head.

"Blue." Gertrude replied.

"It's odd isn't it, every time I get blue. They say the average eye donation is brown or discoloured. But every time I get blue." The president sighed.

"Do you know what I think it is?" Gertrude said, helping the president with his jacket. "There's some old ladies out there who think the president of Yellow Orang-Utan Industries is the young and handsome man they see on TV and they make a personal donation."

"Do you really think so?" The president smiled while he thought about it. He didn't like to associate with other people. He disliked people so much that when he had to be present at meetings, and he had to be present at a lot of meetings, he had a computer image made of someone else entirely to represent Yellow Orang-Utan Industries. Everyone thought that the computer image on the screen was the president of Yellow Orang-Utan Industries, the most powerful company in the world. People didn't mind though, Yellow Orang-Utan Industries could fool little old ladies into giving up their eyes for a fake image created for PR convenience because they were none the wiser. The real president wasn't as dashing and handsome as his digital representative was, he was a small, wrinkled man with hardly any hair, yellowing, flaky skin, gangly limbs and, what he thought was a very embarrassing penis. He watched Gertrude tie his shoe-laces and proceeded down the hall. The time was eleven forty-two.

At twelve O' nine the president of Yellow Orang-Utan Industries put another spoonful of noodles in his mouth and stared into his cup. He looked up and stared at Gertrude sucking on a bright pink ice pop.

"How many market hackers have we got to talk to today?" he asked. Yellow Orang-Utan's digitally manipulated president was enabled to convene internal communications with Yellow Orang-Utan staff, including contract negotiations. Alternatively the president could throw the work to a team of the company lawyers. Doing these interviews personally just ensured the real president didn't get too bored. Gertrude removed the ice pop from her red lips. She looked at her clipboard nearby.

"Twelve or fifteen. Depends on how much they want and how much talk that'll take." She resumed her icy activities. The president looked at the noodle cup he held in his hands, he stirred the noodles slowly. White noodles and the brown warm liquid that comforted them. A lone noodle floated on the surface of the whirling brown goop. The president recognised it, it was an alphabet noodle, the letter C.

"I suppose they'll all want money as per usual," he said, a little loud to get above the sweet sucking noises of Gertrude's pleasant lunch. Her ice pop was melting and bright pink fluid was dribbling down her chin and fingers.

"Enjoying that are you?" The president responded, with a grin. Gertrude smiled and at the same time tried to keep her mouthful of pink juice from gushing out. She swallowed and put the ice pop down on the table.

"I don't think I want the rest of this." She said, wiping her mouth and licking her fingers.

"Mmm. Me neither, I'll just finish this and then we'll invite those hackers in. Call someone in to clean this lunch up."

"Yes sir." Gertrude replied as the president took one last gulp from the cup and looked down into it. There was just a little brown muck left and the alphabet noodle C. It shouldn't be in there.

"Call the first one in Gertrude." The president said as a cleaner entered the room.

"Yes sir," Gertrude replied, and she retreated to a small console she had as a workstation adjacent to the president's quarters, it included a secure computer that included a common scheduling program used by the many employees at Yellow Orang-Utan Industries. She began pressing buttons. The cleaner began to wipe at the president's boardroom table, where he and Gertrude nearly always took their ordered lunch.

Eventually the first hacker arrived. He dressed in a similar style suit to the president, only a different colour.

"Hello Zigfried, have a seat," the president said, pointing to the chair Gertrude had occupied at lunch, the cleaner was giving it a quick wipe. Zigfried sat down and Gertrude handed the president a document with Zigfried's details. He eyed it with care.

"You've been with us for quite some time now Zigfried. Do you wish to stay with us or are you retiring?"

"No sir, I am definitely not retiring," Zigfried said with a grin. He was relatively young, with black hair slicked back, and only early signs of bags under his eyes.

"Good," the president said, and continued. "I understand your contract permits you to retire at any time you wish, and you've worked here long enough to secure a generous pension. And, while still working, every year you are permitted to address your pay for that year. So are you happy hacking the market with us here at Yellow Orang-Utan, or do you wish for more compensation this year?" The president eyed Zigfried the way most mega corporation owners have a tendency to eye their employees. He knew exactly what Zigfried was going to say next. All the contractors were the same. Money was all they cared for. A while back a whole bunch of contractors would demand custom built limousines, not these days though. It was money or nothing. It was a lot easier to deal with, which was why Yellow Orang-Utan Industries preferred and acquired a whole lot more contractors than any other company. This was also because they could afford to employ more contractors than any other company.

"Every year I am entitled to a pay rise or other benefits of some type. I wish to increase my yearly pay to fifty five billion pounds," said Zigfried. The president glanced up from the documents he held in his hand. The document didn't say he normally demanded this much money, a little higher than most contractors. The president sighed and thought about all the other contractors that he was to see today.

After the umpteenth contractor, the president allowed another hacker in. This one would be very different. This one was a freelancer, a young hot shot, not yet shepherded into a long term contract like the majority of market hackers. Gertrude buzzed him in. This one was younger than Zigfried and had a giant mess of hair. He dressed slackly like a lot of young hot shots did. He looked about very early twenties and indeed was, according to his document handed to the president by Gertrude. Not an implant on him it seemed. That would change, so would this freelancing business. The man's name was Wellington.

"All right Wellington, what can Yellow Orang-Utan Industries offer you to stay with us this year?" The president asked, a little tired.

"A black card," Wellington replied, a little frankly. The president looked at him with a start. Freelancers could demand odd things, this made them a little more fun to haggle with than the O' so many contractors. The president smiled at him.

"I hardly think that you have enough money to be eligible for a blac-"

"Not that type of black card, the other kind. The kind that deals with laws. The get out of jail free card." Wellington said, not a touch of humour on his face.

"Are you in trouble with the law Wellington? We at Yellow Orang-Utan will ably assist you with a top lawyer if that ever happens."

"No," Wellington replied, "I just want a little more freedom. I have a list of laws here I've selected, and a black card should give me choice over them." He handed the president the list. The president gave it a quick look. It was rather elaborate list of rather petty crimes, nothing too serious or extravagant as fifty five billion pounds.

"This looks easy enough for us to supply. I trust you don't expect everything. We'll do what we can. I'll have it organised and sent to you in a week or two." The president said to Wellington, who still looked dead serious.

"Thank you, sir," Wellington said, cheer returning to his face. He stood up and walked out, waving to Gertrude as he did. She didn't wave back. The president thought about the C noodle he found in his noodle cup earlier that day. His thoughts drifted into thoughts about clouds, and Gertrude.

"Shall I call the next one in?" Gertrude's call interrupted the president's idle thoughts. The president peered up at her, there seemed to be a little irritation in her face.

"Yes-yes," the president tiredly replied. Gertrude walked to the door and pressed a few buttons and hurried back over to his desk to give him the document on the next market hacker.

"Last one," said Gertrude, with a delightful grin on her face. The president smiled back, it was nearly home-time. The president peered at the document.

"Oh, Si'ng!" the president exclaimed, feelings grew inside him, reminding him why he bothered with in-person negotiating each year. Si'ng took a while to arrive but soon he was in the office and the president was beaming.

"Hello Si'ng how are you?" the president asked.

"Fine, I suppose," Si'ng answered. The president's feet were tapping against the floor.

"And the kids, still doing well I take it?"

"My eldest's buddy got him a green card, haven't seen him since." The president laughed a little but then looked at Si'ng and realised there was nothing funny about it. The president stared into Si'ng's face; it looked very old and feeble.

"This is one of the years you get to talk about your stay here at Yellow Orang-Utan. If we can make your life here any easier, we will happily do it," the president said, like he was talking to an employee.

"Sir," Si'ng began, "I have been with this company right from the start, it seems. I have served what seemed loyally for nearly forty years and I am the longest serving contracted market hacker at Yellow Orang-Utan. Which is why I think I am deserving of this request. I wish to be cryogenically frozen for fifty years. While I am in suspension, so too will my contract be. When I am thawed, I shall resume my work here at Yellow Orang-Utan until my contract runs out. I want the freezing to be entirely discreet and I want no-one to know." Si'ng looked very tired and a little ill. The president looked at the sad old man's face. He thought about the merry atmosphere that had been surrounding him not ten years ago. Something that felt like guilt wallowed in the president.

"Alright, tomorrow it shall be done," the president said. A small smile slipped on and off Si'ng's face.

"Thank you, Sir," Si'ng said and stood up to leave. "Give my regards to the president."

The president watched him go and thought about his mother, his mother who thought he was dead when she died. He thought about how amazing it was that after all these years at Yellow Orang-Utan, Si'ng still believed that the president was that almost idiotic face on the Telly-net screens. He thought of the C noodle in his noodle cup. His mind wandered and then he looked up at Gertrude. She was looking at him oddly, merriment similar to that of Si'ng's old faces accompanied hers.

"Hometime," he said. The time was six forty-three.

After watching some television, the president of Yellow Orang-Utan Industries drifted off to sleep thinking of jigsaw puzzles. The time was eleven O' four.

2.

There is a time when the operation of the machine becomes so odious, makes you so sick at heart, that you can't take part; you can't even passively take part, and you've got to put your bodies upon the gears and upon the wheels, upon the levers, upon all the apparatus, and you've got to make it stop.

- Mario Savio, 1964

"Good morning sir," was Gertrude's call. It was nine fifteen. The president mumbled back incoherently.

"What do you want to do today sir?" Gertrude asked. The president shot up from under the bed clothes.

"Coffee!" he shouted, his face red. "Why on Earth do you always asked that silly question. What do you want to do today? Phooey. First I want coffee." Gertrude squatted down and handed the president the sweet, black, warm rubbish. The president sipped at it slowly and stared up Gertrude's skirt.

"You have a PR meeting this morning," Gertrude replied, standing up and brushing her skirt's creases.

"Gertrude?"

"Mmm?"

"Why do I have a PR meeting today? At ten thirty in the morning? That is very early. Normally PR don't set them so early." The president looked up at Gertrude's lips. Gertrude let out a small cough.

"I have news," she said. She walked around the president's bed and picked up the remote control. She flicked on the Wall-span television. The president watched the faces on the news site. He listened to what the television had to say. He saw the loud jacket the man was wearing. His mouth dropped open. The time was nine sixteen and thirty seconds.

At ten twenty-six the president of Yellow Orang-Utan Industries was yelling rather loudly at some employees of his company.

"What do they mean he's dead? How can this happen?" Were some of the things the president of Yellow Orang-Utan Industries shouted at the employees. the employees looked scared to answer.

"We think it'll be very good for sales," one remarked.

"It was the best time to utilise such a situation," another blurted.

"What situation? How the dickens can a computer image be dead?" the president of the biggest company in the world cried. An employee of Yellow Orang-Utan Industries stood up, they seemed a little excited.

"When they say a man answering Piano Smedley's description was found dead in the street, they literally mean a man answering Piano

Smedley's description was found dead in the street. A real actual physical body. We didn't pay them. We didn't make it up. It really happened," He tried to explain.

"So what, so some idiot clubber had himself implanted to look like me. . .Or it, to be precise," the president snapped.

"So what happens is, we go and confirm it really is Piano Smedley, claim the John-D.O.A. body as ours, and bang! Instant Diana!" said the employee, almost singing. The employee seemed to enjoy his work.

"Excuse me, what happens when the perceived successful owner and creator of the biggest company in the world dies? What subsequently happens to all the investors? They run away. Killing off Piano Smedley is extremely stupid. Asinine! How did you lot really think it was going to work?" The president was getting a little angry.

"Sir," another employee began, "the current media attention this is receiving and the media attention you were getting, years before your tragic demise is sufficient enough to work according to the Diana formula. You could make gigantic amounts of sales. Say to ensure investors they're still safe we could tip them off a little. A lot of our current competition have used the Diana formula before and understand quite well why you would 'off' a company's owner." The employee sat down, she still seemed a little afraid.

"I would like to be alone for a few minutes. I want to fume. All of you get out and don't come back without the numbers," the president said, looking at his feet. They all trundled out, a little more excited than they were at six that morning. Gertrude got up to leave as well.

"Not you, Gertrude," the president commanded. Gertrude sighed and sat down on one of the giant chairs surrounding the president of Yellow Orang-Utan Industries, removing her jacket. The president looked up at Gertrude's arms and absent-mindedly licked his lips. The time was ten thirty-two.

At ten fifty-five the president was back in bed again, snugly in his happy place. He sniffed the scent of his stale body odour, nearly gagged, then sat up. A lie-in wasn't the solution to having your public image die. He reached for the remote control device and noticed Gertrude was playing some silly computer game on the Wall-span telly. The volume was off but there was still the giant whirring that Wall-spans liked to hurt your ears with when you turn them on.

"Turn that off!" The president grumbled. Gertrude turned and looked at him with a mischievous look. She put down the console remote and stood up.

"Sorry. Awake so quickly? I hadn't given you the blindfold shot not thirty seconds ago," she said.

"I felt sick," was the president's reply, "pop the news-feeds on?"

"Yes sir." Gertrude changed channels, feeling awkward. Was the death of Piano Smedley making her feel uncomfortable? All her friends at the media-bar would be crying and having the millionth-zillionth drink in tribute by now. But the media-bar had never interrupted the way she worked. The extra-curricular event would be the likely highlight of the week, but Gertrude did not feel good.

   The president slumped back in his bed. Gertrude slumped back against the wall. Suddenly she was struck by the static of the Wall-span. It hurt. The Wall-span television was an enormous high resolution screen that would put many cinemas to shame, but its electrical workings across such a large surface created a hazardous amount of residual static electricity. To touch it could be quite a shock. Gertrude had just bumped her head against it. She struggled with the shock as the electricity went through her body, her head felt like it had exploded, her chest hot, her heart palpitating strongly. The president hadn't noticed.

   "Fetch me some clean sheets and send these to the cleaners, Gertude, they stink," was all the president had to say. Gertrude had doubled over, but had yet to cry out. She was sure the president couldn't hear her. She fought her head out of the static cloud and took in deep gulps of air. She stumbled, her legs felt nowhere near a proper ground level. She wheezed. She felt around for her inhaler and took a puff of delightful chemicals.

   "Gertrude?" the president called.

   "Right away sir," she managed. Regaining some composure, Gertrude visited the president's large walk-in robe where there was a shelf for clean bed sheets. The president had no idea the scale of his collection in there, Gertrude picked out a lot of his clothes for him, leaving others by the door to the robe for the president to grab when she wasn't around. She brought out the sheets to the bed. The Yellow Orang-Utan president stood by the bed, hands on hips, looking useless. Gertrude began to remove the dirty sheets. The bed, like the sheets, was custom built and enormous. As she tugged on a large stretch of satin, Gertrude lost her momentary composure. The pain of the electric shock was still lingering, Piano Smedley's name repeated itself on the news-feed, echoing in her head.

   "Excuse me," she said quietly and scurried to the nearest bathroom, the president's own.

   Gertrude wiped a tear off her face, looked at herself in the bathroom mirror and began to cry. She looked up at her sobbing face and buried her face in her hands, again, and then once more. When she felt she'd calmed down, she reached for her make-up case to reapply her make-up. When the job was new, and carrying its own stresses, this was more common, and she'd learned to paint on her composure, quickly and seamlessly. That was happening less, this was different, this had caught her off guard.

   She watched the compact case scan her face with its tacky, cute, pink laser. She looked at her face in the mirror, and watched another tear appear and work its way down her face. The make-up applied itself to the tear. A glossed-flesh tear marked its way down her face to Gertrude's chin, spoiling the application. Gertrude put the case in the bathroom sink and leaned on the counter shakily. She looked at herself in the mirror as another tear emerged and began its journey. She slumped to the floor and cried again. She sniffed and wept and thought about Piano Smedley. The president finally thought something was wrong. He'd moved to the bathroom door and could hear Gertrude's sobs. He knocked.

"Gertrude...It's me...Can I come in?" he called, and Gertrude heard him. The ugly man was trying to comfort Gertrude, or at least attempting, to begin, to try. He was the man who'd had news-media inform his own mother that he was dead and that a young Piano Smedley would now be the president of Yellow Orang-Utan Industries. Gertrude burst into another wave of tears.

Hearing the sobs, the president had another go at knocking on the door, then walked into the bathroom. He was wearing a satin robe. His mouth dropped open when he saw Gertrude's forlorn body slumped depressively on the floor. She looked up at him with a tear-strewn face. His gaze made another dart at her panties.

"Gertrude, Gertrude what's the matter?" The president said, trying very hard to make Gertrude feel better. He leant down and put his smelly, saggy and bony arms around her. He made a stupid attempt to rock her like a child.

"I...I got zapped by the Wall-span," she sobbed. She wouldn't tell him the real reason.

"Well are you alright? Can I get you anything?" Gertrude could smell the president, he stank.

"A glass of water or something? Huh? Should I get you to Dr. Westaway?" Gertrude quickly stood up and threw up in the sink, all over her compact case.

"System error," the make up case said. The pink laser shone through Gertrude's breakfast and the applicator tried in vain to paint it glossed-flesh before it realised there had been a system error and shorted.

"Oh no! Your pretty case, here let me help you clean it." The president spoke in his most caring voice, which was quite caring. He grabbed some hand wipes and wiped the sick into various smudges on the hot pink leather case. Gertrude, looked at her puffy eyes in the mirror, touching nothing. The president looked up from the compact case which he was diligently wrecking and stared at Gertrude's sad face.

"Tomorrow, if you're feeling better, would you like another body sculpt? A massage perhaps. Would you like that?" The president asked with an encouraging grin.

Gertrude smiled childishly. She thought of Ted Showbiz, the fat man at the media bar, how drunk he would be tonight if she saw him.

"Yeah." She whispered. She wiped away her last tears. The time was eleven twenty-nine.

3.

The dreamers ate popcorn and hawked and spat, or simply snored, while on the screen the creatures of Hollywood, wonderfully preserved cadavers, acted out the fantasies of their masters.

- Riverside Drive, 1962

At eleven O' five the following day an employee of Yellow Orang-Utan Industries came bouncing into the president's quarters.

"Good news sir!" The employee cried. The president of Yellow Orang-Utan Industries looked up from his computer console. The Diana effect was kicking in. Today was going to be a good day.

"Yeah, tell me something I don't know," he yelled back at the employee, grinning. Today was going to be a good day.

"Sales are up, and we've broken a number of interaction records across popular telly-net platforms with Piano Smedley content," the ecstatic employee piped, nearly giggling. Today was going to be a good day.

"Oh yeah," the president exclaimed. He was reading through an onslaught of e-mail, that's what he would do all morning and some of the afternoon, after that Gertrude would be back with a new bit of synthetic wonder. Today was going to be a good day.

The president stared at the screen and clicked away with the mouse, trying to identify the automatic spam from the personalised condolences. Extra staff were helping manually filter communications, but they struggled to stay ahead. Extra staff were on the ground floor of the Yellow Orang-Utan Industries building dealing with the thousands of commiserating flower deliveries. Sales had just broken records a minute ago. Today was a good day. The time was two minutes past twelve.

At four thirty-three the president of Yellow Orang-Utan Industries' stared at Gertrude's naked body, firm and perfect everywhere. She danced about in front of him, giggling with medicated glee. The surgical scars were rapidly disappearing as the doctor sprayed them, soon there wasn't a mark on her. The doctor blabbed on and on and pointed to her back a lot, the president's head swam

"Well, what do you think?" Gertrude asked, once the doctor had exited. It took at least a minute for the president's brain to register what she was saying.

"Uh-uh, uh-it'sss fantastic!" he eventually stammered. "Once again, a true masterpiece for the pleasurable benefit of mankind. A wonder. Proving the timeless point that Gertrude can, and will, get better. To the world," the president toasted, raising high a glass of bubbly wine that sat nearby. Gertrude giggled and curtsied.

"Thank you, sir," she said childishly.

"Can I take you to dinner tonight ? You can show off your wonderful new ah-?"

"Back?"

"Thank you yes, your lovely new back at *The Swinging Hanky*?" The president asked with a little hopeful air. A lot of the time Gertrude would go clubbing at night and it didn't leave much night-life left for the two of them together. Gertrude gave him a smile, as she buttoned up her shirt.

"Why certainly, Mr. President," Gertrude said approvingly.

"Thank you, Gertrude. I'll have you picked up at eight. You can go home now. Good afternoon." The president waved as she left the room and he hurried off to have a very cold shower. The time was four fifty.

At eight O' nine Gertrude and the president sat down at their table at *The Swinging Hanky*. It was well attended that evening with it's sublimely rich customers. One particular customer had arranged to move in. He permanently occupied booth four with all his business surrounding him doing what one would normally do in an office, and lying back when sleepy in the comfortably accommodating booth seat. He'd prefer to own his live-in restaurant, but the current owner doesn't want to sell probably the only restaurant with a permanent resident, it was a mutually complementary stalemate.

Gertrude stared at the overweight man who lived at the restaurant. Her eyes wandered about the room and stared at all the men, there were a lot of overweight men in the restaurant. Before her work at Yellow Orang-Utan, she'd only heard of these *Swinging Hanky* customers from a sex-worker friend. Gertrude hadn't believed her, but now she found their excesses droll. She looked across at the weedy man on the other side of the table. He appeared to be the only guy in the room that hadn't a cosmetic implant, & maybe the smallest. Despite a drunk exhibitionist dressed a little like Carmen Miranda a few tables away, he definitely stood out. It was odd how he was also the richest man among all these loud drunk men, and had the least dominating body language. The president of Yellow Orang-Utan Industries smiled from behind a menu.

"What are you having?" he asked Gertrude, who hadn't picked up a menu at all, having only just managed to stop staring at the drunks and gluttons.

"Some fish," Gertrude answered as she picked up the laminated cardboard booklet. She hadn't actually found a fish dish on the menu to speak of. The president was looking at the menu with watering facial features. He wiped his nose and said: "I think I'll have the turtle, that clone meat is simply divine."

When the waiter came they both ordered a clone fish dish with random salad. While they waited they attempted small talk but the president of Yellow Orang-Utan Industries was feeling intimidated by all the loud business people and Gertrude was feeling depressed. The anaesthetic from earlier that day had worn off, she felt like the same old fool getting her clothes off for her employer, and the funeral of Piano Smedley was on the Telly-Net that night, it kept returning to her mind. Conversation soon died away.

A tall, burly man approached their table, he was looking really friendly.

"Hey there, Arty," he chirped. He called everyone Arty.

"Hey, Magnum," the president replied in a friendly greeting. They shook hands and displayed to Gertrude a collection of token male greeting body language.

"I can't believe you're getting away with it you ol' dog!" Magnum exclaimed, "Where do you get off pulling that old trick? I trust you've been watching the Telly-net?"

"You know what, I really haven't, I've been reading all of Piano's obituaries and e-mails nearly all day, I haven't seen much at all, and filtering all the spam along with it is a full time job." The president replied with a really smug air.

Gertrude decided to ignore these men. She thought about getting zapped in the static cling of the Wall-span. Her head still felt sore from the memory. If dinner didn't take too long she might go to a club tonight and get some endorphin pills and go to a therapist in the morning. She could still feel the panic and sickness dwelling inside her body from the day the news broke. She looked at her time piece. The funeral was starting now. The computer animators had been awake for days on cartons of wakey shots creating the frames for the procession. Somewhere in the hidden recesses of the Yellow Orang-Utan building, they had created an all fake funeral, full of fake mourners and fake paparazzi surrounding the grave site and the church. Tomorrow the fake viewpoints and pictures from their fake cameras would be in the Telly-net and press.

Magnum had got a little serious as the conversation continued. He left very quickly with a: "See-ya Arty, until Mr. Smedley rises from the grave to sue the pants off ya!" and a wave. Then Gertrude proceeded to go on ignoring the president.

The food arrived but Gertrude slipped off to the toilet, her journey surrounded with fat rich men. The food looked good enough to eat, the president dug in. He slurped and sucked and chomped through the perfect clone meat. He waved a waiter over to ask about the salad. The waiter pressed the button on his note taker for a random salad. Numbers on a small screen whirred and glowed red until there was a click where then, they glowed green. Gertrude returned to eat and the waiter returned with a potato salad. The president stopped chewing and made a face, he didn't like potato salad. Lately there were poison epidemics breaking out on the news linked with potatoes. The dead pink turtle flesh wallowed in his mouth, the taste began to turn sour.

"I hope you like potato, the random salad has appeared to have turned on us," the president said, indicating the oily white assemblage. Gertrude smiled.

"No," Gertrude replied, "I've never tried it."

"I heard the epidemics were found to be caused by poor processing procedures, perhaps they can make potatoes properly now." They both eyed the potato, it seemed to distract them entirely from the succulent meat in front of them. She dug a spork in and walloped a lump of the salad in her plate. From a far corner of the restaurant, Gertrude heard a gasp of surprise.

They ate and ate the delicious fish dishes. Chat began to intrude the feasting. Bottle tops, Telly-net, bad Telly-net, carrots, cooking, tennis and the associated balls, freelancers, Wellington, and his black card.

"Do you suppose he knew who the president of Yellow Orang-Utan was?" The president asked, after politely swallowing.

"You talk as though Piano really was the president ." Gertrude said, thinking again of the live-cast funeral.

"Most everyday people seemed to believe. Even Si'ng thought he was. I wonder if Wellington thought so too. I mean, a lot of the kids his age had Piano accompany their teenage years, they grew up with him in the media. He made their lives easier through Yellow Orang-Utan. Do you suppose he believed in him?" the president asked. He'd stopped being the real president of Yellow Orang-Utan Industries a long time ago. Now his only job seemed to be making sure everyone believed that the fake was real so he could get richer. Everyone else worked for and believed in Yellow Orang-Utan Industries. He just presided over the money.

The president took a mouthful of potato salad to his mouth. Someone in the back of the restaurant prepared to leave. The president looked at Gertrude, waiting for a reply. Gertrude didn't answer, tears welled in the back of her eyes. The time was nine twelve.

At nine fifty-three, Gertrude strode into the media bar she knew all too well, *Fishpaste*. The place, covered with wall to wall Telly-net monitors in lots of clever designed spots, was one of the most popular clubs in the district. The walls were screens, the ceilings were screens, tables, stools, and even the bar was an elongated thing with a stretched picture format. She spied some friends in a booth on the wall farthest away from her. They spied her, and waved. She walked over to them, they all looked glum. The club had a glum and depressed feeling to it. The giant and dwarfish screens that plagued the bar all showed images of Piano Smedley's funeral. Gertrude sat down in the booth with her friends. They all wallowed inside their various drinks and personal screens and paid little attention to her, except Mumford. He moved close to her and expressed care.

"I cried three times today, what about you?" Mumford asked Gertrude's neck, from Gertrude's shoulder, where Mumford's head rested.

"Twice," she answered, reluctantly. Ted Showbiz, the bar's regular booze hound was lying in the middle of the floor, doing some odd sort of interpretative dance, some other mourners were joining in. Everyone in the entire bar was looking sad. Gertrude felt very out of place.

"You smell freshly chopped. Have you had an implant?" asked a voice from Gertrude's shoulder. A small smile crept on to her face, the only smile amongst the booth, and amongst the club.

"You can tell?" Gertrude asked, feeling the afternoon's cheekiness reviving momentarily.

"Yes," Mumford answered, "I can always tell if anybody's had one, it's my keen sense of smell. I look forward to seeing your latest improvement." Gertrude felt warmth where Mumford was resting against her.

"How about tonight, I could do with someone's company. It's been a bad day." Gertrude said. Mumford looked into Gertrude's eyes.

"I can't," he said, "at least, not while everybody's grieving. I'm not in the right mood. Look around, nobody is. Even Ted Showbiz wouldn't be up for it." Ted Showbiz was too drunk to even laugh at. Gertrude's cheekiness quickly dropped away. She had been trying half the day to hold back tears, grateful for the distraction her cosmetic surgery had offered, but the club was about to usher in more tears. The fake funeral was playing before her eyes, every flat surface displayed the manufactured images. Her eyes welled up.

"Sensae." Gertrude whispered across the table that her speechless friends sat around. A head rose from its position of staring into a glass of pink scotch.

"What?" asked Sensae. He was a stupid man, with dark hair. He had a habit of wearing sunglasses of interesting colours. Not today. You could see his eyes, all puffy from crying.

"Have you got some endorphins?" Gertrude asked from across the table.

"I know what you're thinking and they don't work. Besides, this is hardly the time," snapped Sensae. Gertrude felt a tear roll down her cheek.

"Please," she pleaded. Sensae threw a small bag of sweet smelling pills at Gertrude.

"Take them and leave me alone," he grunted. On a wall opposite the booth a woman burst into a fit of tears. Ted Showbiz got up off the floor and went to comfort her. Gertrude, with some difficulty, got out of the booth and hurried to the toilet, as another tear made its way across her face.

When Gertrude emerged from the toilet, the woman was still crying. Ted Showbiz had started crying and so had a bunch of others. Group grief. She walked a little way across the floor, towards her friends who had also started to cry. Sensae was right when he said the endorphins wouldn't work. She was beginning to cry anyway, in the middle of the club's dance floor. The drugs just made the crying feel more dramatic, she looked down at her feet and felt embarrassed. She remembered the time when she got drunk and told them that Piano Smedley was only a computer generated image. They hadn't believed her. Her grief seemed fraudulent in comparison. A tear fell before her feet, with a glossed-flesh taint. She ran out amidst sobs. The *Fishpaste* screens continued to play the Piano Smedley funeral. The time was ten twenty.

At ten forty-one the President pressed a button on his remote control and the Wall-span TV's image flickered away. He chuckled to himself. He had just watched Piano Smedley's funeral and couldn't believe his eyes. He looked for his phone that was to be by his bed, unforseen circumstances had taken it to a nearby wall.

"Drat," said the president. He looked down at his stomach, it had a few cookie crumbs on it. He brushed away the crumbs and left his comfy bed to fetch the phone.

"Hello Windle?" The president asked after he picked up the phone and placed a call.

"Yes mmm, Windle here. Who's calling?" Windle replied.

"Ah Windle, the President here. I'm just calling to say that I enjoyed the funeral immensely and I want those computer kids to get big fat bonuses and let them know their work is appreciated a great deal here. I had my friend Magnum Ndgali call me earlier and he told me his Telly-net had never before had so many visitors to his site. He had to upgrade while the thing played, he was in a state of emergency it was that popular." The president said to the telephone so that Windle could hear.

"Right, got it, big fat bonuses. Can do sir...So that's it, nothing more I can do for you sir?" asked Windle thoughtfully.

"No Windle, that will be all," replied the president.

"Alright then, Good Evening Mr. President," Windle said.

"See-ya Windle" the President of Orang-Utan Industries said as he hung the phone up.

The president carried the phone back to his bedside and put it down. He crawled back into bed and, for a while, tried to fall asleep. He couldn't, being too excited about the funeral and the implications of the money he could make with this new scheme. He got out of bed again and tried to calm down. He wandered over to a window in his room and looked down. He was up very high, it had been a long time since he last looked out of this window. He saw all the lit windows of the neighbouring buildings. The offices below his bedroom, in their windows he could see their lights on. Sometimes the lights weren't on but the computers were, he could sometimes see screen savers blinking and flashing. Some of the lit-window places still had people in them, despite the time of night it was. They were probably hard working employees pulling all-nighters for some important meeting in the morning. He saw a young woman and a young man working earnestly side by side, he fantasised when they'd stop and have it off right before his eyes. The president soon lost patience.

The Yellow Orang-Utan Industries building had an elevator on the outside of the building, it was mostly a ride for tourists to get a kick out of, but a few employees used it from time to time. The president thought about going down to the floor of its highest destination, he could ride it up and down for a while until he got tired. Then the president had a better idea.

The president put his head against the glass and leaned on it, the window gave way and curved itself around the president's bald head and the surrounding tiny flakes of dead skin. He pushed further into the glass, the gel glass curved and bent out towards the night sky. He pushed himself into a twisting, emerging bubble of magical plastic, surrounding light swirled and moulded itself around the president's view. The president hung there in mid air, suspended by the window and looked down into the street. He could see all the lights and cars on the street. The bubble stretched and distorted the light so the lights hundreds of metres below took on a completely different form in front of the president's eyes. His blue eyes, his new eyes.

The president levitated in the bubble for a little while longer, until he started to feel tired. His thoughts drifted to Gertrude dancing naked in front of him that afternoon. Then he felt short of breath in the bubble. He pushed against the soft plastic that moulded to his forcing arms. He kicked himself free eventually and soon got mouthfuls of air that he gasped at gratefully.

"What a rush!" The president of Yellow Orang-Utan Industries exclaimed to himself. He sat on the floor of his bedroom, the gel window slowly remoulding itself into an ordinary pane. It was an expensive experimental luxury that also provided an intense and sudden feeling of bliss and fear all at once. That's why he had the gel window installed. He remembered how upset Gertrude had been the day before when she'd got zapped in the static. The gel window now had only a small ripple where he had first set his head against it, and his gaze set on the Wall-span. As extravagant as the gel window was, the president sometimes preferred the dangerous side-effect that came with his enormous television. Getting zapped by the static gave him a buzz, a buzz that reminded him of caffeine, of brokering important deals, of being a powerful figure in the world of business, where once upon a time, he'd developed a brand called Yellow Orang-Utan. The president stood up and walked excitedly towards it. He put his back up against it and pushed upwards with his feet. His head swam as electrical current rose in his head. He felt nauseous, but his thin stick figure held up. The president couldn't breathe, he took off his robe. He felt the electrical field buzz around him, his ears hummed as he removed his underpants. Naked, he pushed himself off the TV and fell to the floor. He gasped for air and felt exhilarated.

As he regained his breath and his sweat cooled the president, stood up and saw his reflection in the Wall-span. A sad looking man with shocking posture and bony arms, and a near-invisible penis. He sighed and thought about Gertrude. He had a good, hard think about Gertrude, naked, nipples erect, moaning. After that he had a good hard think about pornography, old pornography, new pornography, pornography with Gertrude in it. He looked at his small, limp penis and sighed rather disdainfully. The president returned to his clothes and crawled back into bed. He was soon fast asleep. The time was eleven seventeen.

4.

In this way economic theory has managed to transfer the sense of urgency in meeting consumer need that was once felt in a world where more production meant more food for the hungry, more clothing for the cold, and more houses for the homeless to a world where increased output satisfies the craving for more elegant cars, more exotic food, more erotic clothing, more elaborate entertainment – indeed the entire modern range of sensuous, edifying, and lethal desires.

- The Affluent Society, 1958

At nine twenty, Gertrude walked into the president's bedroom to wake him.

"Good morning sir," she said. Gertrude glared at the lump on the bed, there was no response.

"Good morning sir," she said once more. There was still no response. Gertrude found an orthopaedic chair made of wood by the door, which she sat on. She watched the president of Yellow Orang-Utan Industries sleep for around five minutes while she applied some make-up. Her head felt a bit woozy from the endorphin pills she had taken the night before. The president rolled over and grumbled in his sleep.

"Good morning sir!" Gertrude called loudly. The president suddenly shot up.

"What?" he cried in a confused state. Gertrude stifled a laugh.

"Oh, it's you," the Yellow Orang-Utan Industries president said, disappointedly. Gertrude went to ask what he'd like to do today, but then she remembered he didn't like it much.

"I suppose I'll have to have a meeting today to see what's to be done about all this money being thrown at us. Won't I?"

"Yes sir." Gertrude rose from her chair and tried hard to look official. The president crawled to one side of the bed and put his feet on the floor.

"Very well, help me get dressed." The president sighed. The time was nine twenty-eight.

At nine fifty-one the president sat looking at his computer. Writing to be read, lots of it, by him. Propositions, sent by e-mail, propositions for every piece of rubbish ever produced to be endorsed by Piano Smedley, or his likeness. Commemorative statuettes and plates to be sold with stamps issued by the post office. Record producers wanted rights to the official Piano Smedley soundtrack. The official Piano Smedley biographical film, the official Piano Smedley juice bar, Piano Smedley shoes, Piano Smedley pizza, Piano Smedley shampoo, the list went on and on. The president decided to get someone else to read this and sort it out without him. The Diana effect was kicking in. Today was probably going to be a good day. The time was ten O' four.

At ten forty-seven the president sat amongst his bubbly employees. Gertrude sat next to him. She was just as happy as the employees. They talked and talked and talked. The chief subject was speculations about what to do with the money. The president sighed to himself. The employees were far too excitable, they hadn't had this much money to play with before. The president was the richest man in the world, the amount was irrelevant, he always had enough to play with. The bubbly employees started making jokes. The amount of money they were making was ridiculous. They laughed, loudly. Gertrude laughed too. Then one stopped and apologised.

"It was wrong of me to laugh at a time like this. I'm sorry sir, I'm sure you knew Piano well." The president looked at the apologetic employee. It was odd for somebody to acknowledge the old man, he'd kept a low profile and hadn't said anything since he'd got there. Most of the time the president just murmured and nodded a lot. He smiled.

"I'm sure if Piano was around right now, he wouldn't mind at all. Not in the least," the president of Yellow Orang-Utan Industries replied. Gertrude looked at the president, he tried very hard to listen to the employees' ideas since the employee's apology. He felt included now, but was losing interest. They were more talking amongst themselves than to him.

"Yes. I like that one, go with it," The president of Yellow Orang-Utan Industries said suddenly.

"But I haven't finished yet," the relevant employee said, surprised at the interruption.

"Oh? Well, I think you're on to something. Prepare a report for me to read by tomorrow, get some help if you need. I want formal reports from you all in relation to these fantastic ideas you've had. This has indeed been a successful brain-storming session. I'll see you later," concluded the president gruffly. The employees sat for a while looking stupid. As the resonance of the president's words faded inside their heads, they got up and left. The president continued sitting in his chair staring at the glass wall, with the glass door which the employees had all just exited from. Gertrude also sat in her chair, waiting for the president to say something.

"Shall we go now sir?" she asked eventually.

"No, I think we'll just stay here for a bit," the president of Yellow Orang-Utan Industries replied. They sat in silence for quite a while, nothing happened. The president licked his lips once as he thought of lunch, but that was it.

Finally someone walked past the glass door. It was Wellington, he was dressed in black. He didn't appear to notice them behind the glass door.

"Who was that?" asked the Yellow Orang-Utan Industries president.

"Wellington, from market hacking," Gertrude replied.

"Oh yes, I remember now. That kid with the black card. You waved to him when he came to the office the other day," the president recalled.

"No, he waved to me. I didn't wave to him," replied Gertrude.

"Oh, I see, shall we go now Gertrude?" The president asked considerately.

"Yes," Gertrude said as she rose from her chair. The two of them left the room with the glass wall and proceeded up a hall. The time was eleven thirty and forty-five seconds.

At twelve thirteen the president and Gertrude sat in the president of Yellow Orang-Utan Industries' boardroom and ate some lunch. Gertrude didn't have a bright pink ice pop today, she had a salad. A salad that wouldn't melt and dribble all over her red lips. The president had noodles in a cup again. This time there wasn't a C noodle in there by mistake. They both ate in an uncomfortable silence. This time there wasn't friendly chatter, the way they had friendly chatter at dinner the night before. Their thoughts were elsewhere and personal.

"Is there another meeting this afternoon?" asked the president of the biggest company in the world.

"Yes," answered Gertrude. "The public relations types are desperately seeking a spokesperson to represent the company, now that Piano has gone." She was trying very hard not to show an emotional quiver when mentioning Piano Smedley, who was only a computer generated character.

"Well they can't have me, can they? I died years ago. I had loads of media attention too, nothing compared to today's standards but pretty considerable to say the least," the president replied.

"Well, they'll be here soon so we should get ready, shouldn't we?" Gertrude suggested while swallowing a mouthful of chewed lettuce and capsicum. The time was twelve twenty-four.

At one fifty the public relations types finally entered the president of Yellow Orang-Utan Industries' boardroom. They looked a little flustered, people rarely visited the president's boardroom.

"Sorry you had to wait so long, a little communication muddle I'm afraid. Do sit down," the president said. The PR types did so. A small, secretarial type stood behind them, wiping her nose.

"Sir, it is imperative at this point to have a face to take the place of Piano. We will lose investors unless the public can be happy with another spokesperson." A PR person said, rather quickly.

"I'm aware of that," acknowledged the president. "But we can't be sure that another fake will work as well as Piano did. All the other companies which tried it failed miserably. It was luck, as well as help from you in public relations that enabled us to have Piano work for us so successfully for so long."

"But sir, you must take into consideration that the team that designed Piano Smedley are still working for you, they are still quite happy working for you and they certainly won't defect. They haven't worked for anyone else in ten years, it's in their contracts. If they could do it then, they can do it now." A rather stern public relations type said, as the secretarial one sniffed and tried hard to stifle a burst of tears.

"Excuse me," she said, and ran out of the boardroom. The Yellow Orang-Utan president watched her leave.

"What's the matter with her? " he asked.

"Poor dear can't cope. She grew up with Piano and, well for some reason she grieves the poor boy's death." A more flustered of the public relations types answered.

"But she's just been in here, we've been talking about how he was a fake and all!" the president exclaimed.

"I know I was trying to talk her out of it most of yesterday afternoon. In between brain-storming sessions and such. She just doesn't want to come around." A blundering PR person replied.

"Well, I'll be damned," exclaimed the president softly. "Back to the point I was about to make, you are correct as far as the quality of my computer creative team, or whatever they are called, is concerned. But they have indeed been with me for ten years, that's an incredibly long time for these computer whizz-kids. We've been hiring new teams for the past five years. Not to mention the fact that they aren't outgoing socially, nor as savvy with current trends as the PR teams." The president's prattle carried on out of Gertrude's earshot before she followed the grieving colleague past the obtuse wooden door. The small secretarial type sat looking even smaller, hunched in an orthopaedic wooden chair. She cried and cried.

"It's unfair isn't it? They act like it's all a normal routine don't they, but it's different isn't it?" Gertrude said, as she approached her.

"I-I-" the secretarial type attempted to say before crying again. Gertrude comforted her.

"I feel the same way" she said, stroking the poor girl's quivering back. Gertrude squatted by the crying secretary in the wooden chair for a good while. Soon the crying fits calmed down.

"What's your name?" Gertrude asked the secretarial type.

"Biscuit," said Biscuit.

"It's a horrible feeling isn't it, Biscuit? Everyone else is grieving, but everyone else doesn't know better. They don't-"

"People call me Biscoe," Biscuit interrupted.

"Oh," Gertrude replied.

In the boardroom, the president was being told why he shouldn't try being the public image for Yellow Orang-Utan Industries again, and feeling a bit stupid for suggesting it in the first place.

"It isn't economically viable, nor is it good PR," a public relations type said.

"Ever since the Bill Gates fiasco no one has had someone as old as you, Mr. President represent their company, not ever," warned a clear thinking public relations type who could remember back to when the president himself represented the company.

"Especially since you had yourself killed to raise profits!" Another public relations type mentioned, rather quickly. The president sighed again and swivelled in his comfy chair. The public relations types shut up and watched him spin.

"Look just use the vice-presidents for a while, focus on just Naamah Nelise if you want to. We'll get to it later. You can all go now." The president said, indicating the obtuse wooden door. The Yellow Orang-Utan Industries public relations staff ventured outside the boardroom. They passed Gertrude and Biscuit who were sitting on identical orthopaedic wooden chairs and discussing, between the occasional sob, where they would eat for dinner. Biscuit got up and went with the public relations staff.

"I'll see you at seven then?" she asked.

"Definitely," Gertrude replied as she rose to greet the president again.

"Ah, there you are, Gertrude," the president said as she entered the boardroom. The time was three thirty-seven and forty-five seconds.

At twelve past eight, Gertrude and Biscuit finished their meal at the *Stale Sun Screen* restaurant. It was to be a family restaurant that would eventually franchise. However, its inner city location somehow caused it to be a hangout for sarcastic arty types, it became a mix of waiters in candy pink outfits and roller skates, and customers who wear a lot of black and occasionally scribble beautiful poetry on the colourful, chequered walls. For this reason, it never became as franchise-able as the owner-manager hoped. They settled in to warm after dinner drinks and spoke for a good long while about the way they both felt about their genuine grief for a false icon of big business.

"It's just that we grew up with his image on the Telly-net when we were so young and he's like part of our memories," Gertrude explained.

"Yeah, but unlike some of the other stuff we lived around, like Photo Dolls, Piano never left our life when we grew up," Biscuit added.

"Well, Photo Dolls were still around when I left Uni, but I suppose they just weren't the same. I mean, when you grow older you realise how goofy those dolls are, but Piano wouldn't seem to change in quality like other stuff." Gertrude said, while having a sip on the warm coffee she held in her hand.

"Mmm, that's right," Biscuit agreed, swallowing a mouthful of her herbal tea, "he seemed so, so genuine, you know?" They both paused for a bit. A tear welled in Gertrude's eye. A few sprang from Biscuit's ducts also. They looked at each other wiping their tears and laughed a little. Their gaze held while Gertrude moved closer to Biscuit.

"I hate them for this," Biscuit said, a little angrily.

"Who?" Gertrude asked.

"Those Yellow Orang-Utan people, it's their fault. They exploit everyone's love for this great guy that they've dangled in our face for all these years. I mean did you see everybody on the day of the funeral?" she asked between sips and sobs. Gertrude lit a small stick of incense that was on the coffee table in front of them. Biscuit continued.

"And it's worse when you know that these people are being fooled. We're supposed to detach from it at work, we know he's not real but we just can't help it. It's not fair that they play with our emotions like that. Someone ought to drag the real guy who's responsible for it all out of his big penthouse at the top of some skyscraper in Montevideo, or wherever the hell he is, and put him in the stocks, or something."

"I'm not angry at them, it's part of what a big company like that does. They exploit everybody, all the little people, they always have and I think they always will. It's still very effective business, even if it isn't all there, ethically," Gertrude replied.

"But don't you think when they provide for us in such a way and the way they nearly 'Mother' us through the media, you don't think they have an obligation to treat us properly?" Biscuit said, an argument slowly stirring.

"No," Gertrude replied, the incense smoke wafting about her head, "people have got to understand that they are simply a company out to make money, creating icons that people relate to and even love in a bid to increase sales is an acceptable and good form of busine-"

"-But it's the fact that people fail to realise this, that this character is a marketing ploy, that makes it wrong," Biscuit said, interrupting.

"No, it's the fact that the person they created isn't real and they never told us that", Gertrude stated, trying to collect her thoughts, "people have the ability to think for themselves and realise that the ploy is indeed that, a ploy, it isn't wrong. But I think when they deny us the truth that the ploy we've loved isn't a human being capable of real emotions, they aren't being fair. We should have a right to know what's real and what isn't. What they are really exploiting are people's irrational emotions." There was a bit of silence for a while between them. They sipped, but a lot of the sobbing had stopped as they began to address the questions circling in their heads.

"Well if the exploitation of our emotions is the main problem, whether he was fake or not isn't the issue," Biscuit began, "so what is it exactly that we have fallen victim to? Have we had our emotions exploited? It's easy to tell with all the other people that have."

"I think It's different for us because we've worked for the people that dish out all these ploys. But we can't help winding up on the receiving end now and then, especially when we were young and growing up without the knowledge we have now," Gertrude offered, "but when Piano died, I realised just how much attachment I still have for him, fake or not. It's working with the people who invent the ploys, treat them the way people really should treat them, rationally and sensibly, that you forget your own feelings for this ploy."

"Our failure, is still holding on to our beliefs with emotions that aren't found in business circles? That just shows you how insensitive these business types are, they are inhuman," Biscuit said, her anger at those business people growing further.

"I've worked with Yellow Orang-Utan for nearly my entire career," Gertrude began, "and it came as a shock when I heard that Piano had died. It really did. It upset things, I had to accept that Piano was fake on one level, and I guess I just about had. But the shock totally broke through that level. This guy I saw all the time when I was a little girl, who I sort-of accepted wasn't real has suddenly stopped existing. It was a big change to cope with. I guess it opened the door to all the subconscious emotions that I had denied myself while working for Yellow Orang-Utan."

"They just won't ever understand, they detach and don't have emotions," Biscuit said. They both sipped their drinks, which were both nearly empty now. The stick of incense had burned down considerably.

"I don't think I feel entirely the same way you do though, Gertrude," Biscuit added, "because I never really accepted the fact he was fake. They would keep reminding me he wasn't real and everything, but that wasn't working. It just made me angry that they failed to be emotionally attached to this character, even more so when he died and they just sat around talking about the implications of the death to Yellow Orang-Utan Industries. I think I'm also angry at myself for not accepting it."

"I feel stupid," said Gertrude. They finished their drinks, ordered more and talked for another good long while on other subjects, until they finally left the *Stale Sun Screen* restaurant. The time was eleven twenty-two.

At nine fifty-five, earlier in the evening, the president of Yellow Orang-Utan Industries received a phone call from a man by the name of Magnum Ndgali.

"Hey there Arty," Mr. Ndgali exclaimed at the beginning of the phone conversation.

"Howdy Magnum," the president replied, sounding tired.

"How are you doing? You got your tech-boys working overtime for the next Piano?" Magnum asked, like an eager little child. The president wasn't paying much attention to Magnum Ndgali, he had his Wall-span TV on, volume off. He was distracted by the image of a small time businessman trying to sell an odd electronic gismo. The Yellow Orang-Utan Industries president was trying to guess the businessman's ancestry, but he couldn't educate his guess unless he turned the sound back on, which would be rude when he's on the telephone. Instead the president tried to pay attention to both Mr. Ndgali and the second rate ad on the telly.

"What?" the president of Yellow Orang-Utan Industries asked.

"I trust that's what you're doing, making another Piano. A bigger, better Piano Smedley?" Magnum said, he had an ability to make anything he said sound exciting even when he didn't use adjectives.

"Uh, actually we're not all that sure yet," the president replied. He had the ability to make himself seem smaller than he actually was when he used his voice.

"Oh," Magnum Ndgali said, excitedly. He hadn't expected that kind of answer. There was a short silence between the two corporate head honchos.

"We-we are about to begin some marketing of Piano merchandise though. The offers have been pouring in," the president stammered. At this point the conversation drifted away from business matters and became a bit lude. Magnum Ndgali was a bit of a braggart, and a sexpot. He told stories of carnal conquests while the businessman on the Telly-net caught the president's attention again.

"Mmmm, mmm hmm," and, "oo-oh yeah" was all the president of Yellow Orang-Utan Industries said for the next nineteen minutes or so. Gradually Mr. Ndgali's voice became irritating to the Yellow Orang-Utan Industries president.

"See-ya Arty, just remember I'm an investor over there OK?" Magnum said eventually, much to the president's relief.

"OK Magnum I'll see you around," the president said with a friendly tone of voice, which made him sound small, "Bubbye." With that the president hung up the phone.

Irritated by Mr. Ndgali's sex stories, the president found some pornography on the Telly-net and watched that. He turned the volume on and became bombarded by the sounds of five naked, painted ladies having orgasms. He hurriedly reduced the volume and watched the program until his lack of arousal grew to unbearable levels. He found again the Telly-site with the small time businessman trying to sell his electronic gismo. With the volume on, the president of Yellow Orang-Utan Industries realised what a brilliant invention it was. He picked up the phone. After only one ring, Windle picked up the receiver of his telephone.

"Hello, Windle here," the president's phone receiver said.

"Ni Hao Windle, the president here," said the president.

"Ah, Mr. President, what can I do you for?" Windle said, which the president heard his telephone say at the very same moment.

"Well Windle, I'd like you to buy a company called Dinosaurs 'R' Us, they sell a great little gismo with a candle and a watch battery. You can't miss it." The president of Yellow Orang-Utan Industries ordered.

"Can do sir. Will that be all sir?" Windle asked, through the telephone.

"I think that's all, thanks Windle," the president replied.

"Alright then, good evening Mr. President," Windle farewelled.

"See-ya Windle," the president said into the phone, before hanging up. The time was eleven O' seven.

At midnight the two women walked along the street that contained Biscuit's apartment. A taxi had delivered them to the street and Gertrude would continue to ride in the taxi in about five minutes. They walked closely together, occasionally varied parts of their anatomy would brush against each other softly.

"Gertrude," Biscuit was heard to say.

"Yes, mmm?" Gertrude was heard to reply.

"Will you sleep with me tonight?" asked Biscuit. Gertrude

the heterosexual began to feel a little self-conscious and a little worried that Biscuit was going to do something a bit confronting. Biscuit held Gertrude's hand.

"It's a really emotional time for me, and you too by the sounds of things. I could use some late night company," Biscuit explained.

"Um," said Gertrude.

"The frustration this whole Piano thing causes me makes it worse, you understand don't you?" Biscuit looked hopefully at Gertrude.

"Biscoe, I'm sorry, but I'm not a lesbian." Gertrude said, carefully. Biscuit graciously let go of Gertrude's hand, removing any slight unease created by the physicality.

"Oh, Good night then. It was a very nice evening," Biscuit said with a very friendly tone.

"Goodbye," Gertrude said, proceeding now to the taxi. She got in the taxi and rode away, waving and smiling at Biscuit. Biscuit watched the taxi disappear from view and stood for a while outside her house.

"Um", Biscuit said. The time was twelve O' six.

5.

Thus, rational behaviour is perceived as leading to an act of purchase on the basis of appropriate information gathering and processing, even if this is within a broader perspective than utility maximisation and, indeed, may be taking place unconsciously.

At seven fifteen in the morning the president of Yellow Orang-Utan Industries surprised himself by being conscious and unable to go back to sleep, even at this early hour. He crawled to the edge of his bed, dragging with him the cocoon of satin sheets that was keeping him snug and turned on the Wall-span TV. He found a Telly-net site with computer games on it and began to play the games. The games looked marvellous on his gigantic television screen. The colours, the sounds and the terrific graphics sometimes made the president drop his jaw in delight. He pressed his keypad buttons vigourously and watched the results. After a long session of playing computer games, Gertrude came into the room, her body looking shiny. She sat down beside the president and began to play computer games too.

"Good morning sir," Gertrude said as she pressed a red button nine times in a row very quickly.

"Good morning Gertrude," said the president as he held down a green button and made the TV emit a whooping sound.

"What do you want to do today sir?" was the question Gertrude asked.

"Well Gertrude, I thought I might attend that meeting where they are going to show me all the Piano merchandise they are going to market soon. After that I believe some PR people and myself are going to venture carefully into the computer lab and give a little instruction on what our next Piano is going to look like," the president of Yellow Orang-Utan Industries replied, promptly.

"I thought you weren't sure you wanted just another Piano?" Gertrude said.

"Well, that's true, but I'm hardly what you'd call up to date in business affairs to know what's best for Yellow Orang-Utan anymore, am I?" the president countered.

"I suppose not," Gertrude replied. They continued playing computer games until they both got hungry and decided they wanted to eat breakfast. After breakfast they sat about for a while in comfortable chairs.

As it was her wadrobe's regular day to do so, Gertrude wore a very short dress. By this time of day the president should have ogled her in that very short dress at least a dozen times. He had not done so. Gertrude looked at the president suspiciously, who wasn't looking at her at all. She coughed and crossed her legs a couple of times and not once did the president eye her and start to drool a little. The time was ten forty-seven and thirty seconds.

At eleven O' clock the president, Gertrude, some designers, a public relations officer, a market hacker and some of the executive directors sat at a rather long table and watched strange and silly items that were part of the Piano Smedley merchandise machine appear from a humming contraption and proceed down the rather long table along some sort of conveyer-belt. There was a little doll that talked. There was a series of nice looking photos of Piano Smedley, that were fake. There was a mobile phone that rang. There was colourful fabric, rolled up neatly. And a large roll of film, that was a documentary, that was also fake.

"These are the official Piano Smedley products," said the public relations officer, "these will be distributed to most major shopping malls and large retail stores. They will also be available in the inner city boutiques and trend stores." A few executives applauded. The rest of the room studied the assortment of Piano Smedley paraphernalia for quite a long while. The president of Yellow Orang-Utan Industries looked confusedly at the colourful objects. He was quite sure he didn't understand why they were supposedly such good quality products. They were supposed to be classy? He didn't mind however as he assumed that the people in marketing and public relations knew what they were doing.

Suddenly the items were taken away. The whirring contraption at the end of the rather long table began to move and shift again and more items came out of it. These were even stranger and sillier items than the ones before. They proceeded down the conveyor belt. There was a small plastic figurine, that wasn't painted properly. There was a T-shirt bearing Piano Smedley's image on the front, that said I DON'T REALLY CARE on the back. There was some toilet paper, that looked cheap and of the scratchy sort. There was a mouse trap, that made no sense. And a blow-up Piano Smedley sexual aid, that had a remarkable resemblance, really.

"And these are the unofficial Piano Smedley products," said the public relations officer, "these will be distributed to small time markets on the outskirts of suburban areas and in some major shopping centres overseas. They will also be available in discount stores in various places about the country." One executive director applauded. The market hacker applauded too. People at the table talked excitedly, a few looked at the products. The president had no idea what was going on. He stared bluntly at the bizarre products that sat atop the conveyor belt, that had slowed to a stop on the rather long table. He began to have a feeling that the people in marketing and public relations didn't know what they were doing. The chatter continued.

"Excuse me," the president said, pulling aside the public relations officer, "what is with these unofficial products? I don' t understand why we made them."

"Well sir, if we've learnt anything from the Disney corporation is that if we bombard the public with too many positive images of our logos, certain members of the public question their integrity. It happens with all manner of public figures who only endorse good publicity, a mockery made of their name through the production of B-grade products. We've foreseen that with the attention the media gave to the death of Piano Smedley, there will indeed be a backlash against him by the same sort of public members that buy the infamous Mickey and Minnie sodomy dolls. To avoid the production of merchandise that may discredit Piano's good name, we hope to corner the market ourselves with these products you see here." The public relations officer said.

"But won't these discredit Piano's name?" The president of Yellow Orang-Utan asked.

"No sir. Despite their B-grade appearance, each product has been carefully designed to be sold, but not for longer term use. The blow-up Piano for example, although the intentions of those who would normally buy a blow-up doll are often for somewhat lewd behaviour, the Piano Smedley doll has been designed to be, er, less appealing for that kind of behaviour and it's likely the purchaser will throw it out," explained the public relations officer.

"My, isn't that clever, Gertrude?" the president exclaimed to his personal assistant.

"What?" asked Gertrude, who's mind was thinking of anything other than some of the horrible toys on the table.

"That doll, that blow-up Piano doll that no-one will want to have sex with. Isn't it ingenious?" The president explained.

"Yes," Gertrude replied. The time was eleven twenty-five.

At twelve O' four the president sat with Gertrude and ate lunch. The president had ordered a random salad for himself and it didn't contain any potatoes, which was good. Gertrude ate another ice pop, this time it was a red one. Somehow, the ice pop had a shiny, chrome-like appearance. No matter how much Gertrude licked it, no matter how small it got, it retained its lustre. Gertrude sucked on it with the usual dribbly lips and childish delight. The president did not watch her eat it and focused only on his salad, which contained a large amount of mushrooms. He thought about Si'ng and forks. Gertrude thought about religion, the president of Yellow Orang-Utan Industries and why she made so much noise when she ate an ice pop shaped the way it was. Once they had finished lunch, the time was twelve thirty and twenty seconds.

At exactly one O' clock a small security officer apologised for the company's wait, but explained that was how the security door worked. Directly after that, the president of Orang-Utan Industries, Gertrude, some public relations officers, Biscuit and some market hackers walked into the Yellow Orang-Utan Industries Information Technology laboratory. The computer lab wasn't something people like this often walked into, there were far too many wooden orthopaedic chairs than comfortable spongy ones for a start. The market hackers who stared at computers for most of their job weren't as concerned as the public relations officers, who walked very close together and held the occasional hand. Gertrude was joined by Biscuit and they walked together, a little apart from the others. They were a little concerned about the confronting images of Piano Smedley they might encounter at this meeting.

They of course had no reason to be the least bit frightened. The laboratory was simply a large office with lots and lots more computers than the usual large office. Soon they were greeted by an ordinary looking, middle aged man named Pepito. He called himself Pepi and soon directed them safely through the laboratory to a cosy office with a tech boy inside who could create the next Piano's guidelines with his computer and software. Although they passed a scary, non-lit corridor on the way in, the cosy office had warm lighting and a poster on the wall of kittens, everyone felt safe in there.

The public relations officers gave instruction after instruction as to what they wanted the next Piano to look like. Pepito interpreted the bubbly instructions into some sort of jargon for the tech boy to understand. The tech boy took these orders probably better than Pepito took the public relations instructions, as he slowly added in the guidelines that would translate into the next Piano Smedley, until something didn't match the public relations officers' vision and they would have to recompose the image. The president of Yellow Orang-Utan Industries felt very out of place. Sometimes it was hard enough trying to understand what the public relations people were trying to get across, but the translations from PR speak, to tech boy speak, to computer speak was incredible. It was going to be a very tedious afternoon.

Eventually they settled on something, so everyone eventually was pleased. A nice, friendly looking bloke who wore a cool red shirt was going to be the new fake president of Yellow Orang-Utan Industries. The president's eyes hurt from looking at the screen. He hadn't even noticed that Gertrude had left the room with that public relations secretary a good twenty minutes ago. He realised it when they popped back in while Pepito shook hands with the tech boy, who was flustered after this long session of dealing with people who didn't really understand computers. A bunch of the public relations officers shook hands and suggested the consumption of bubbly alcoholic drinks. The market hackers who were far more sensible, rational types didn't smile at all. Instead they got on to their calculators and mobile phones because, to whoever on the other end of the line, this afternoon's events really meant something terribly important, sensible and rational.

They all talked a little excitedly as Pepito guided them through the scary dark corridor and out of the laboratory full of very young boys, a few not as young girls and at least one thousand computers. They smiled at the small security officer who made them wait another two and a half minutes before he would open the door. He apologised for the company's wait as they filed through the door at exactly three forty-five.

At about ten past three earlier that afternoon, Gertrude and Biscuit sneaked quietly out of the small, non-offensive office and stood in the dark and scary corridor.

"That was a bit too much for me," declared Biscuit.

"I don't like those PR types much," added Gertrude.

"Well you don't have to work with them all the time like I do. I can't imagine you like that little weedy man you always have to work with," Biscuit said.

"That man...is the president!" Gertrude whispered, a small grin spreading on her face.

"No?" Biscuit cried, quite astonished. They both looked at him through a thin window that looked into the small, non-offensive office.

"Well I never. I always supposed that he was just one of his flunkies or something. And you have to wake him up every morning and such?" Biscuit asked with a large dose of curiosity kicking in.

"Yep," Gertrude replied. They both continued to look into the window, the president looked completely dumbfounded, which Biscuit found very amusing.

"And has he ever, you know? I mean, it's kind of sexy being that powerful. Have you? Or anything?" asked Biscuit. Gertrude indicated her dress.

"These days I just gotta dress like this a lot. He pays for all my implants and he gets to watch the whole process. All he sees is me naked for a couple of minutes, he can't bear watching the operations." They watched the president wipe his nose on the back of his hand.

"Although a long time ago, when I first started, he liked to touch me a considerable amount. Soon after that he told me to give him a couple of lap dances, one went a bit far, but his drive has died off these days. Now it's just implants about every seven or eight months," Gertrude said.

"So, he was the real president, the one who was the real, proper president when Piano was the, other president?" Biscuit asked.

"Yuhuh," confirmed Gertrude. Biscuit soon stopped asking questions about the president. They saw the computer screen in the non-offensive office. They didn't like the image on it. Biscuit stopped looking at it. Gertrude slowly began to stare at it with an odd sense of curiosity. She thought of something.

"Biscoe, you don't suppose if we watched that guy being made we wouldn't feel the same about Piano anymore?" Gertrude asked.

"I like the way I feel about Piano, he's dead and I'm sad. I'm just like all my regular friends who don't work for these horrible exploiters," Biscuit replied confidently, "I guess it's just a belief that I hold on to, the same way all those bartenders all over town like to believe in mythical creatures like mermaids and satyrs. I feel more human this way."

"Suit yourself, I still feel stupid about it," Gertrude replied. The sound of some weepy music filled the air. They looked to where the sound came from and there above their heads was a screen that was playing the Piano Smedley fake funeral.

They quickly left the dark and scary corridor and went into one of the nearby offices that were full of wooden orthopaedic chairs and computers, and a few very young people. The very young people who could sit in orthopaedic chairs all day and work with three or four computers at once, comfortably. They were paid nearly as much as the market hackers to do so. At one point an investigation was made into how young exactly the people the big businesses were hiring in the computer technology department of their corporations. It didn't lead anywhere, because they were immensely happy with their employing company. In this office Gertrude and Biscuit were away from some of the more disturbing images in their previously inhabited rooms. A small teenage boy looked at them awkwardly. They looked at him right back and he resumed his work with his two or so computers.

"How many implants have you had since working for the president?" Biscuit asked with a low voice, so as not to be heard by the teenagers amongst the mass of technology. Gertrude looked at her body.

"I think I've lost count," she bragged. Biscuit looked at Gertrude's body too.

"I can see why," Biscuit added, "I've only managed perfume ones so far." Gertrude declined to ask what scent, she looked at Biscuit's legs, they were smooth and shiny, pale and supple.

"Hmm, nice," Gertrude said. She began to think more about the process she had watched through the office window.

The adolescent children ignored the two women entirely. They spoke to their computers, which were very obedient. Command after command flowed from the children's lips and fingertips, the computers would beep accordingly. Biscuit and Gertrude stood against a wall and talked a little amongst themselves. They soon stopped talking when the behaviour in the room gradually fascinated them. The dozen or so teenagers talking to glowing screens, occasionally making an emotional noise of pleasure or frustration, when their computers would behave well or poor. Biscuit realised they were standing next to the light switch. The light in the office wasn't on, but the room glowed from the computer monitors. Biscuit nudged Gertrude and with a grin, turned on the fluorescent lights.

"Oi!" a dozen or so teenagers yelled.

"Oh, sorry" Biscuit said cheekily, turning the light off again. The two women giggled as they left the office and proceeded back up the dark and scary corridor. They looked through the doors leading back to the small non-offensive office and realised that behind most of them were more offices full of young people and computers. They returned to the non-offensive office and hid at the back where they wouldn't see anything. Pepito shook hands with the tech-boy. The time was three thirty-eight and thirty seconds.

At three forty-two that afternoon, after all the market hackers and public relations officers, Gertrude, Biscuit and the president of Yellow Orang-Utan Industries had been led through the dark and scary corridor, and the computer laboratory with a thousand computers and nearly a hundred children, as the corporate party waited at the security door to the computer laboratory, Wellington walked across a foyer. Biscuit turned and noticed him shuttle across the grey-pink carpet. She did not know who he was and paid little attention to it. If Gertrude had noticed she would have paid attention to it. Gertrude was quite sure that Wellington was a market hacker. Wellington had not been with the other market hackers this afternoon while they all stood staring at the screen in the non-offensive office. This would have occurred to Gertude and she would have spent a long time wondering what he was doing in the computer technology department when he didn't belong there. She would not have asked him why either, as she did not like speaking to him. But Gertrude did not notice Wellington in the foyer, Biscuit did. The security door opened and the time was exactly three forty-five.

At eight fifty-three that evening, the Yellow Orang-Utan Industries president went to the *Greenacres* Telly-net site and selected program number thirty six, which he enjoyed watching. He searched sites until he found a site selling the infamous Mickey and Minnie sodomy dolls. When he saw them he turned off the Wall-span television promptly. Disgusted by what he saw, he questioned himself as to why he even had the intention of finding out what they were. He sank inside his gel window for a while until he realised how bad he smelt and went into the bathroom to take a shower. As he stood in the cubicle and the accurate laser searched his body for bits of oils and dirt, he stared at the bathroom floor where

Gertrude had wept and wept. He continued to stare when the laser stopped its amazing operation and the shower cubicle beeped six times. He got out of the shower and put some pyjamas on. He went to bed quietly. The shower beeped six times every half hour because the president forgot to turn it off. He ignored the insisting beeping and fell asleep. The time was four past ten.

At three sixteen early that morning the president of Yellow Orang-Utan Industries awoke with a start, cold sweat beaded on his forehead from a horrible dream about a time-bomb. He groaned because he didn't at all like being awoken when he wasn't ready, he also abhorred horrible dreams. He became infuriated when he discovered, half an hour later that his shower was still beeping, with the near identical beep to a time bomb. He got up and turned it off and went back to bed. The time was three forty-seven and thirty seconds.

6.

Hmmm, an invisible wall.

At nine fifteen in the morning, the president sat in his cocoon of warm satin sheets, the static clinging to him like a big teddy bear giving him a hug. He heard his door open and footsteps walk towards him on the floor.

"Coffee!" snapped the president.

"Yes sir," the voice of Gertrude replied, and her footsteps promptly left the room. When Gertrude returned and gave the president of Yellow Orang-Utan Industries his demanded coffee, she asked "What would you like to do today sir?" The president muttered something under his breath and then said: "The market hackers and the public relations people are going to have a meeting today to discuss what they are going to do with the new Piano Smedley's character and personality when he starts making public appearances. I'll have to sit in and act like I have something important to do with the whole scheme."

"Oh?" Gertrude asked, a little surprised by the way the president put it. The president sipped his coffee.

"Well, I suppose I do pay them," he despondently added. Gertrude was staring at the president a little. He continued to sip his coffee until he caught Gertrude's gaze.

"I'm in a very bad mood today Gertrude. I had a bad dream last night, which makes my bad mood even worse," the president of Yellow Orang-Utan Industries explained, "now will you please help me get dressed? I'll eat breakfast shortly." The time was nine thirty-two.

At eleven thirty-two the president sat down with some of the few people in the world who were aware that he was the Yellow Orang-Utan Industries president, the richest business man in the world. Business men conducted business, which he was quite sure he didn't do anymore. He paid other people to do business. He just sat around demanding reports and things, which he occasionally paid someone else to read anyway.

There had been a time when every one knew who he was, when he had nearly achieved the greatness that Piano achieved. He faked his own death because despite all the public relations stunts, he was human. Piano took his place because Piano wouldn't ever pronounce something incorrectly when speaking to somebody intelligent and awfully important, or when he did stuff up something he was saying, (entirely on purpose) he would cover it up with a delightful joke about it that amended the matter and made him seem just as human as the bimbo interviewing him for Telly-net. The delightful joke of course would tighten the bond that was developing between the two so that viewers would begin to feel, they too could have the lovely friendship that the pair had, even though were separated by thousands of kilometres and talking via satellite, and the fact that Piano Smedley was nothing more than an appealing length of binary code. The human president was never that calculated. Piano Smedley was so good that everyone quickly forgot who the old president was. Few remembered, and those who did, remember his fake death. Now he was going to be behind the scenes for the next Piano.

The president of Yellow Orang-Utan Industries sat in his comfortable chair and looked at the ceiling. Gertrude sat next to him and thought of all sorts of other things that really had nothing to do with the task at hand, except Piano. The public relations officers were trying to convince the market hackers that their new Piano was going to have such-and-such in his personality and this would be good for the business. The market hackers would hurriedly point out that such-and-such president of such-and-such company had the same personality trait and his business failed miserably. The public relations officers would complain that wouldn't be any indication because Yellow Orang-Utan Industries would hardly fall under the same categories as the such-and-such company owned by such-and-such president, whatever his such-and-such name was. The market hackers would then shake their heads and tut-tut and start making phone calls on their mobile phones and start sending e-mail messages everywhere. At that point the market would drop and the market hackers would make smug points to the public relations officers as they guided them through the graphs they had on their computers and the public relation officers wouldn't quite understand and they would go away for five minutes and whinge to each other about how the market hackers didn't kick up this much fuss when they were all helping design what the next Piano Smedley was going to look like. The public relations officers would then return and say that now they would want the next Piano to have such-and-such in his personality trait. The president of Yellow Orang-Utan Industries supervised.

This went on for a very long time. It was going to take all day so they all took a break to eat at lunch time, where they ate lunch. It went on for all of the afternoon also and the president of Yellow Orang-Utan Industries became very, very tired towards the end of it. He tried occupying his mind with thoughts of Greenacres and jigsaw puzzles but it was to no avail. The president was having a bad day, and he was bored out of his skull. Eventually it ended and all the market hackers and the public relations officers went out of the room that contained comfy chairs, which they had occupied for most of the day. The time was five forty-six.

At six ten and fifteen seconds Gertrude was dressing the president of Yellow Orang-Utan Industries for his dinner at *The Swinging Hanky*.

"It's weird, you know," said the president as Gertrude brushed some dead skin off the jacket of the president.

"What's weird?" Gertrude inquired.

"That meeting today, there was a point in time when I was doing the same thing they were, and I had a lot less help," the president said, "but I haven't the foggiest notion what they were going on about today. Why is that?"

"You're probably just getting old I guess," was Gertrude's answer to the president's question.

"Huh, I'm as old as some of my contemporaries and they don't have any problem with it. I'm just out of practice. I've plum forgotten!" The realisation hit the president as a weird sensation that made him feel a bit funny.

"That's certainly a possibility," Gertrude remarked as she finished dressing the Yellow Orang-Utan Industries president.

"There, all done," she announced quietly.

"Thank you Gertrude, you can go now." That was the last thing Gertrude heard the president say that day, she straightened her skirt before him and then left the Yellow Orang-Utan Industries building. Her steps made a noise as she crossed the floor and out the president's door. The time was six seventeen.

At eight fifty-nine, having returned home from *The Swinging Hanky* and wrangled himself into bed, the President of Yellow Orang-Utan Industries glanced at a small clock beside his bed and watched the seconds pass. The president went to sleep at exactly nine O' clock.

At nine twelve, Gertrude stepped into *Fishpaste*, and marvelled at the colours and sounds. Time had passed since the death of Piano Smedley, the CGI who made people cry. Every one had mostly stopped grieving too, all the drinkers in the bars were slowly enslaved once more to their biological urges and endeavouring to have a good time again. Everybody waved at Gertrude once they saw her, she was familiar to them and anyone who wasn't, liked to fantasise that they were. Sensae was there in a pair of blue sunglasses that made him appear as though he was sprouting horns out the side of his head, Ted Showbiz and Mumford were there too. Gertrude waved at them, they waved back. The television monitors were there, the music was there too. For the first time in a while, the people in the city were willing to pretend they were genuinely happy and they wanted to dance.

Gertrude danced to music too, she danced with Mumford and occasionally with Sensae or Prudence, another friend she had at the club. She had lots of friends at the club, which made her feel comfortable amongst the dazzling sights and blaring sounds. She enjoyed dancing with Mumford especially because as they danced, they danced quite intimately. Mumford glided his delighting hands over Gertrude's torso very carefully, Gertrude extended her own torso into Mumford's congruous movements. After that, they rested and laughed. Sensae gave everyone at the club some drugs and they were enjoyed by all. Eventually the colours and sounds merged together, things got confusing and Ted Showbiz threw up on the floor, but nobody cared.

Gertrude and Prudence went to another club, drank a lot of warm liquids and talked with artists who stayed up late and black boxes which contained the technology to converse politely with wonderful people such as Gertrude and Prudence. Later, Sensae found them in this other club and they talked for a while. Finally, Gertrude caught a vehicle that would take her home, where she lay peacefully on the bed and fell asleep at one sixteen.

7.

The children, though without schools, subject in the playgrounds to the affectionate interest of adults with odd tastes, and disposed to increasingly imaginative forms of delinquency, were admirably equipped with television sets.

- The Affluent Society, 1958

At nine thirty-four Gertrude, walked into the president's bedroom and woke him up.

"What do you want to do today sir?" Gertrude asked. The president glared at her and did not answer, then his face softened.

"I don't want to do anything today," the president admitted. "I just want to do whatever I damn well please. I think I will spend most of the day playing computer games, one of those ones which takes ages to finish."

"Oh," replied Gertrude. The president of Yellow Orang-Utan Industries scurried over to his remote controls and turned on the Wall-span TV for full effect of the colourful computer games. Gertrude proceeded to an orthopaedic chair next to the president's bedroom door and sat down. Her mind wandered off until the Wall-span TV let out a loud piece of cheerful music and the president made a noise in celebration of his own hand-eye co-ordinating skills.

"Have you thought about retiring?" Gertrude asked, thinking aloud.

"What?" asked the president of Yellow Orand-Utan Industries, eyes focused on the Wall-span TV. Gertrude sat up a bit and looked at the back of the president's bald head.

"You were saying grumpy things about how you don't do anything at the meetings anymore. Why haven't you retired like lots of people your age?" The president's brow furrowed as he half-listened to Gertrude's new question. Music and video emitting from the TV indicated the beginning of the next stage of the president of Yellow Orang-Utan Industries' computer game.

"I don't know," he said, beginning a reply, "people retire when they work for people, but I don't work for people. I don't work for anybody, haven't for years." The president stuck out his tongue in concentration as he pressed a yellow button in something resembling a pattern, it failed to have the desired effect.

"I mean, I am the president of Yellow Orang-Utan Industries, sort of. I'm, you know, the secret one, but the real one. If I retire I don't think it would be mine anymore, and it barely seems mine as it is. It wouldn't exist without me in the first place though, so I reckon I should hang on to it. Why do you ask?"

"What?" Gertrude asked, not really paying much attention to the president's weak answer.

"Why this talk about retirement?"

"Oh, I don't know really. Bit bored I guess." The president of Yellow Orang-Utan Industries frowned at her response and pressed a keypad so that it pressed near painfully into his thumb. The time was eleven thirty-seven.

At eleven fifty-two Gertrude peered at her clipboard. It showed the meetings that the president should be attending that day. She expected that there were probably a lot of phone messages for him, wanting to know where he was and his reasons for not attending this morning's meetings. She predicted that she would not have answers for them. Her thoughts wandered elsewhere when the president called out "it's lunchtime!" Gertrude was startled, it was three minutes and forty-one seconds past noon.

At twelve nineteen that afternoon, the president of Yellow Orang-Utan Industries and his female assistant Gertrude were spooning into their bodies mouthfuls of a delicious and nutritious savoury custard, served in large ceramic bowls. Like peanut-butter sandwiches or rich banana cake, the custard had a knack for sticking to the roof of their mouths. During lunch the president made Gertrude find out how the meetings had gone that morning.

"Well they got nothing done really. They rang me and started complaining that you weren't there and weren't answering your phone." Gertrude said, while pushing with her tongue bits of the custard amongst her upper wisdom teeth, she looked at the president in a way that made him feel irresponsible. Her tongue made a smacking noise amongst her gums. He groaned a bit.

"I don't do anything when I'm there. I don't think they really need me, really," the president of Yellow Orang-Utan Industries whinged.

"I think they need an official to be there, a boss in charge to make it all professional," Gertrude suggested.

"No, it's not that at all. They just don't want to do this job. I mean if they wanted to organise this new Piano thing they could, all the people are there. I mean a market hacker fellow could show up with his agenda and discuss whatever point with the person in PR he was arguing with the day before, I don't need to be there for that. But they don't want to do this job, and so they just use the fact that I'm not there to moan and complain and not actually do anything." They ate in silence for a while, Gertrude got a song in her head and the president tried to ignore Gertrude's smooth shiny shoulders. Gertrude's head was bopping from side to side when the president spoke again.

"Actually I think you're right about them needing an official there to get them motivated. But I'm not prepared to go to any more meetings. I'm fed up sitting there watching them all bickering." Gertrude had nearly finished her bowl of custard, she had eaten faster than the president, who was only halfway through his.

"I mean, one of the reasons we developed Piano in the first place is because I don't want to do this sort of thing. And it's only this interim between the old Piano and the new Piano that I'm at these meetings now. Except now it's been so long that I'm no good at it, and I've lost interest. I mean Yellow Orang-Utan has this really well paid board of directors that never seem to do anything. I can just get them to appear at the meetings and stare at the walls and indoor plants for hours like I do when I'm there." The president of Yellow Orang-Utan Industries said, slopping a spoonful of his lunch back into it's bowl.

"Hopefully we can get this stupid business over and done with. I don't know why we destroyed Piano in the first place. All I had to do for years was press buttons on the Piano software and negotiate a bunch of annual contracts. And the contracts were just for kicks," the president grumbled.

"What are you going to do this afternoon?" She asked the president. The president looked up at Gertrude from his bowl, he swallowed a mouthful of custard before he answered.

"I'm going to keep playing my computer game."

"Oh-" Gertrude began.

"-But now I'll have to contact my board of directors...I'll probably do that toward the end of the day," interrupted the Yellow Orang-Utan Industries president. "I haven't finished my lunch yet though." The president chomped at his spoon and sucked up the custard that sat on it. Gertrude fished for a sweet in her pocket and looked at her clipboard. The time was twelve thirty-nine.

At twelve forty-five and thirty-six seconds the president put down his spoon, Gertrude looked up at him from her mobile phone.

"I want you to take some time off, Gertrude," said the president. A couple of glands in Gertrude's body released endorphins as she looked at him without answering.

"I don't think I'll be doing anything that needs your attention for a while. Windle can take care of basic stuff that needs doing. I'm taking some time off. I'm not going to attend meetings anymore, Hell, I can't even be bothered reading the reports that arrive on my desk at the moment." The president leant back in his chair.

"I'm taking time off," he said, "so you might as well do it too." Gertrude swallowed a mouthful of sugar-saturated saliva.

"With pay?" she asked hopefully.

"Yeah," the president replied simply.

"Thank you very much, sir," said Gertrude.

"Quite alright, I'll ring up the board, then go back to my bedroom and get on with my game." The president rose with Gertrude from the table.

"Can you call in the cleaner please, Gertrude? After that you can have the rest of the day off and I'll call you sometime when I feel like getting back to work." The president ordered as he ambled over to the nearest telephone. Gertrude went over to another communications console and called in a cleaner. The cleaner arrived a few minutes later.

"Hello," Gertrude said to the cleaner with a smile.

"Good day," replied the cleaner.

"Good afternoon, sir," Gertrude called to the Yellow Orang-Utan Industries president.

"Goodbye, Gertrude," the president replied as he looked around for a more useful phone with the speed dial numbers he needed. Gertrude hurried excitedly out the door and into a corridor. On her way out of the building she phone messaged Mumford and her friends to make other evening plans. Twelve minutes later, at one eighteen, Mumford used telecommunications technology to let Gertrude know he could make it to her place that evening and when he'd be there.

At six past one the phone in Jacobo's office rang several times before he answered it. Jacobo was reading a report and felt distracted by the phone ring. He looked up and saw a light flashing on the phone that didn't often flash lately. It indicated it was from offices above his. Jacobo was a member of the board of executive directors at Yellow Orang-Utan Industries, there weren't many offices higher than his. Jacobo jumped up from the couch in his office and grabbed the phone receiver.

"Hello, What do you want to do today?" was Jacobo's greeting. There was a silence on the other end of the phone.

"Hell-?"

"-Is that the way you're supposed to answer the phone?" asked a voice that interrupted Jacobo's second attempt at the phone greeting.

"Er, yes sir," was Jacobo's reply. Jacobo had a shaved head. He wore small suits that occasionally looked restricting, even on his small frame. He looked neither comfortable or uncomfortable today, today's suit was a good median.

"Well, stop it. Listen, the meetings regarding the new Piano Smedley have not been proceeding well and I need you and the rest of the board members to take control from here on in and finalise the project. Have you been receiving the project update memos?" The president asked, thinking he had not sounded this professional for some time.

"Er, I believe Kal-El has been studying those memos," Jacobo replied.

"I'm talking to Jacobo, yes?" inquired the president.

"Yes, sir." Jacobo looked at the helium-filled foil pillow that floated gently in the corner of his office.

"OK, sorry, this is the president."

"Right, OK, I'm used to dealing with Piano," Jacobo said with a smile.

"Well obviously that won't be happening again," the president said with a laugh.

"Of course, yeah. Ummm...so we have to take over the new Piano project."

"Yeah, yeah, I need you to start work on it right away, it should be your only concern for a while. Get those memos off Kal-El. I want you to meet with all the board tomorrow morning at um, nine, to discuss your strategy. I mean your job won't be that complicated, the PR people and the market hackers just need supervision to get the ball rolling smoothly is all. They're a bunch of silly kids really and just need a grown up in the room."

"Uh-huh," Jacobo responded. He was thinking having every single board member meet at nine tomorrow probably wouldn't happen, but didn't want to mention it.

"Tomorrow at nine. What's the deadline for this thing?" Jacobo asked, he was aware that Yellow Orang-Utan had been without a public face for some time now, it was becoming concerning for those paying attention. There was silence at the other end of the phone.

"Sir?"

"End of the month?" The president realised nobody had mentioned a deadline for this project, there foolishly hadn't been one. Deadline pressure could have stopped half the meetings turning to silly squabbles over nothing.

"OK, OK, right. Um, is that all I need to know?" Jacobo looked at the buttons on his shirt and frowned.

"Yes I think so...Ah, all further inquiries should be directed to the vice presidents OK?" The president realised he'd have to contact the vice presidents now.

"Yep, right, got it," was Jacobo's affirmative response.

"OK see-ya, Jacobo," said the president cheerfully.

"Cheerio," replied Jacobo. Jacobo promptly hung up the phone and thought about getting those memos off Kal-El while staring at the half finished report lying open on a coffee table. The table was decorated with the signs of the zodiac, the report covering a seasonal quadrant. He didn't have to read them straight away, it was quite early in the afternoon.

"Karel!" Jacobo called to his secretary in the adjacent office.

"Yes'm?" answered Karel, his head poking through Jacobo's office doorway.

"Could you pop down and get me a copy of the new Piano project memos from Kal-El please?" Jacobo asked, his hands on hips.

"Sure thing," Jacobo's secretary replied, his head disappearing from the door way. Jacobo sat back down on his couch, he picked up his report from the coffee table and rested his feet on the symbol for Sagittarius. His attention returned to the report he was reading before the phone rang at sixteen past one and twelve seconds.

At exactly sixteen past one and ten seconds the phone rang in the offices of Letitia Bjorksdotter, vice president of Yellow Orang-Utan Industries, it was answered by Madison, Letitia's secretary.
"Hello, Letitia Bjorksdotter's office, this is Madison speaking," was Madison's phone greeting.

"Good afternoon Madison, this is the president, can I speak to Letitia please?"

"I'm afraid Letitia's still in Ndjamena, I've been taking messages all day."

"Really? When will she b-" the president asked before being politely interrupted.

"She's due back middle of next week, but that was going to be this week so it may in fact be a while longer." Madison had said this more than once today. The president let out a ferocious sneeze that could be heard through the phone.

"Rrrah! Deary me, sorry," the president said with a sniffle.

"Bless you," Madison responded.

"Listen, I just need to let Letitia know that inquiries regarding the new Piano Smedley project will be directed to her and Naamah OK? That's from now on, starting tomorrow. I've put the board in charge of the project and it should be fine, but if they do make any inquiries I've told them to ask the vice presidents, yeah?" Madison's pink pen scribbled at a handsome pace as she wrote down the gist of the phone message. She began to think about Piano Smedley.

"Uh-huh, well I've got that all down, I'll get that to Letitia ASAP," she said.

"Good, OK, well done. How soon will Letitia get that?"

"I've been forwarding her messages daily, she follows them up in Chad.

"OK, good. I'll see you then," was the last thing the president of Yellow Orang-Utan Industries said to Madison that day.

"Sayonara, El Presidenté," was the last thing Madison, playfully, said to the president of Yellow Orang-Utan Industries. Madison hung up the phone and thought more about Piano Smedley, perhaps more than ever. The time was one twenty-one and forty seconds.

At one twenty-two the phone rang in the offices of Naamah Nelise, vice president of Yellow Orang-Utan Industries. Naamah picked up the phone receiver promptly, she had been looking at something rather dull on her computer monitor and was delighted to have something that could distract her attention from it.

"Hello?" She asked, somewhat cheerfully.

"Naamah?" the voice at the other end inquired.

"Speaking" was Naamah's response.

"Oh, hi. This is the president," said the president. "I'm just calling to let you know that the new Piano Smedley project, which I had been over-seeing myself personally has now become the responsibility of the board of directors..."

"Uh-huh," added Naamah Nelise, secretly not interested.

"...Have been informed to direct their inquiries to the vice presidents. I wouldn't worry too much about that-" the president of Yellow Orang-Utan Industries continued, interrupted.

"-I won't," was the vice president's interruption.

"What?" asked the president.

"I won't worry," answered Naamah.

"Oh...good. Um, right. Yeah, so the board's in charge of the new Piano project, they should be alright on their own. However, if they have any inquiries they have been told to direct them to you and Letitia." The president was pretty sure he'd just said all he needed to to Naamah over the phone.

"Letitia's in Chad" said Ms. Nelise, staring blankly at a small figurine of a cat on her desk.

"I know," replied the president, feeling like he wanted to sigh.

"And that's all?" asked Naamah Nelise.

"Uh-huh. So, ah, goodbye, Naamah," farewelled the president.

"Good afternoon, Mr. President," farewelled Naamah. The respective phone receivers were placed down. Vice president Nelise scowled at her computer. At one twenty-six Ms. Nelise failed to hear the president of Yellow Orang-Utan Industries sigh, he was in another part of the building.

Oakley was talking to someone over the phone and enjoying the conversation very much when at one twenty-seven a little beep went off.

"Oh excuse me, I just got a call on the other line. Could you just hang on a minute?" Oakley asked the gentleman who he had shared a few laughs with via the telephone over the past few minutes. From Oakley's office there was heard a little mumble come out of the receiver he held in his hand.

"Very well," was Oakley's reply to the little voice. Oakley was one member of the board of executive directors at Yellow Orang-Utan Industries. He pressed a button on his communications console, and introduced himself to the new caller.

"Hello Oakley! This is the president," went the president's response, which had a pleased tone. Oakley heard it emanate from the phone receiver's earpiece he held near his head.

"Ah! Good afternoon sir," Oakley answered. Oakley was reputed widely as a pleasant fellow to be with. Today he wore a pink shirt. His smiling face only briefly changed once to a concerned one while the president told him of the new Piano project, and tomorrow morning's meeting. While the president talked Oakley listened carefully while occasionally saying "uh-huh" and "yes". He wrote the details down with a shiny silver pen.

"If you'll excuse me sir, is that all there is? I actually already have another call on the other line," Oakley told the president of Yellow Orang-Utan Industries.

"Not really, just make sure that you get copies of those memos off Kal-El," said the president. Oakley had a very plain office, most furnishings in it were made of pine.

"OK, thanks very much sir, good afternoon," farewelled Oakley.

"Good afternoon, Oakley," farewelled the president. Oakley pressed a button on his communications console and resumed his conversation with the person he was talking to at one twenty-five. There were more laughs to be had between the two, one of them quite hearty. During the remainder of their conversation, Oakley underlined 'Get memos from Kal-El' with six strokes of his silver pen. Some of the time was spent looking at the picture of his wife and daughter, who looked just as happy as Oakley often did. The photo, and it's small pine frame was the only really personal item in Oakley's office. He had never touched the glass in the frame, so there was no fingermarks on it, and it still looked shiny and new.

"OK, goodbye, " was the final thing he said to his friend through the phone that day. Almost immediately after hanging up the phone he called out to his secretary, Palmira.

"Palmira!" He called, "could you go over to Kal-El's office and get a copy of the new Piano project memos. The entire board's supposed to have a copy."

"Yep!" Palmira called back, and popped out of her chair and through her door. Oakley put his hand back on the mouse on his desk and shook away the Yellow Orang-Utan Industries screen saver. The time was one forty-nine and fifteen seconds.

At one forty-eight and fifty six seconds, Palmira arrived at Queenie's office, adjacent to Kal-El's.

"Hi, I need to get a copy of the new Piano project memos for Oakley," she said. Queenie sighed grumpily and rolled her eyes.

"Karel was in here not long ago, for the same thing," she said, as she got out her chair and wandered over to some filing cabinets.

"Apparently the whole board needs copies," Palmira said. Queenie stood by a printer.

"S'pose I should make lots of copies then, before everyone arrives," she said, beginning some mental counting.

The phone rang in Kal-El's office nearby. It rang a number of times before Kal-El picked it up. He was distractedly concentrating on the whereabouts of a paperclip missing from papers he'd just been sorting.

"Hello?" said Kal-El as he picked up a phone receiver.

"Kal-El?" asked a voice belonging to the president of Yellow Orang-Utan Industries.

"Yes. What do you want to do today?" was Kal-El's reply.

"For starters you can stop using that greeting from now on,' said the voice.

"Who is this?" Kal-El asked, a little confronted.

"This is the president, Kal-El," said the president.

"Oh, good day sir," Kal-El replied, a bit taken aback. Kal-El was balding, he often wore a lot of loose fitting brown clothes and always wore a string of beads around his neck. Today he wore a thin suit.

"I understand you're the one on the board keeping abreast of the new Piano Smedley project." The president said with a degree of authority.

"Errr, yes'mm," Kal-El replied. "It's not too healthy is it?"

"No, so I'm putting the board of directors in charge of it now," the president began, "you have your first project meeting with the board first thing tomorrow at nine O' clock. Um, I'm telling the rest of the board to get copies of all the memos made so far off you this afternoon."

"Should I get Queenie to summarise them into a briefing report?" asked Kal-El, interrupting the Yellow Orang-Utan Industries president's spiel.

"Ah it's a good idea, but I think it would take away time we need to concentrate on the project. I mean I want you to focus on this thing, it's the main priority right now. I want this project wrapped up by the end of the month." The president paused.

"What else should I know about this project?" asked Kal-El.

"There's already a lot of people working on it, but you probably already know that. Basically I just want the board to supervise and make decisions when everyone else is squabbling. Apart from that, as of tomorrow, any inquiries you and the rest of the board have should be made to the vice presidents and not me. Right, you're partly ahead of the rest of the board in terms of being up to date with this thing, I'll leave you to finish up your work for the rest of the day," finished the president, who had been doodling a small dog on a pad.

"Okay, thanks very much sir. Tomorrow at nine," Kal-El confirmed.

"See you," farewelled the president of Yellow Orang-Utan. Kal-El returned the phone receiver to its usual place when he didn't talk into it.

"Whatcha up to, Queenie?' he called out to the room next door.

"I'm making copies of those Piano memos," Queenie replied.

"What?"

"Everyone wants copies of the new Piano memos," Queenie called again, trying to be louder than the printer printing.

"Good, I just got off the phone about it," Kal-El called back, looking at a pen on his desk.

"What?" Kal-El didn't bother answering and twiddled his thumbs for a moment. The time was one fifty-six in the afternoon.

At one fifty-seven the telephone rang in Rahel's office and Rahel answered the ringing by picking up a telephone receiver and talking into it. Fortunately it was the correct receiver of the three she had on her desk. One had stopped working and she had meant to get rid of it, yet it remained on the desk to this very day. She had previously been reading some cartoons from a website she often visited, they were similar to the other cartoons that adorned a pinboard on a wall of her office.

"Good afternoon Rahel, this is the president," Rahel heard the president say through her telephone receiver.

"Oh, good afternoon sir," Rahel answered. She dressed rather plainly in a grey skirt and a conservatively coloured striped shirt. Her hair was very neat and she never let it grow past her shoulders.

"There's a meeting for the board tomorrow at nine. I'm putting you all in charge of the new Piano project. You should keep up with all the memos, Kal-El's got them all if you haven't kept copies-"

"I have kept copies, they're still all on my computer since they were sent." Rahel interjected, while hiding the cartoons on her monitor display with the press of a button.

"Oh...good. Well I suppose you're already as informed as Kal-El. You know there's not much work to do on it. But it's just a matter of getting it done," was the president's response to Rahel's information.

"Yep."

"So, nine O' clock tomorrow and please direct any enquiries to Letitia and Naamah, not me," the president of Yellow Orang-Utan Industries said.

"Yep." Rahel answered and then made a quick check. "You want all the board members to meet tomorrow morning?"

"Yeah that's right, at nine," replied the president.

"You know Sabra's on her way to Singapore? Don't you?" Rahel asked.

"What?"

"She left this morning," was Rahel's next response. She heard the president swear.

"Well who ever can be there I want them to be there tomorrow at nine," the president said grumpily.

"Yep, sure thing," Rahel said with a grin. The president of Yellow Orang-Utan Industries and Rahel ended their phone conversation that day with corresponding 'goodbyes' before they each hung up their telephone receivers. Rahel resumed reading the cartoons she had accessed before answering the phone call at one fifty-seven. One of them she found hilarious and she responded with an explosive belly laugh, only her thinking of Jacobo could calm her breathing down. The time was two minutes past two.

At two O' seven that same afternoon the phone rang in Sabra's office, not far from the offices of the other board members of the Yellow Orang-Utan Industries' executive directors. After a number of telephone rings her answering machine beeped and activated the message she left for anyone trying to contact her at her office while she was in Singapore. The machine recorded the responding message the president left, which mentioned his expectation of a present secretary and his intention to try the mobile number mentioned in Sabra's former message. The machine beeped a few times more and then stopped. The time was two O' nine and ten seconds.

At ten O' clock at night in a different time zone to the rest of the Yellow Orang-Utan board of directors Sabra sipped her glass of water. She was looking at a screen bearing information regarding the company building she was visiting in Singapore. Nearby lay a book, face down and open to the last page Sabra had read in it. A steward passed and picked up the empty food tray that also lay near Sabra, Sabra mumbled something appreciative to her. Sabra wore a comfortable and elegant olive-brown pantsuit as she watched the steward's legs walking up the aisle in their cheap stockings. The foetus growing inside Sabra shifted slightly and she looked down at her belly and lay a hand on it, taking another sip of water. Unnoticed by Sabra, something beeped in her handbag. The time was one past ten, almost two.

At thirteen past two, just after Taggart hung up the phone from a conversation with his lawyer, the phone rang again. Swearing, Taggart pressed the speaker-phone button. He had a headache and wanted medicine.

"Hello," he said gruffly, his brow furrowing further up his balding head. A drop of sweat trickled down it and on to his stubbly cheek.

"Hi Taggart, this is the president," announced the president. Taggart shifted in his chair, he hadn't changed his clothes for while and his white shirt smelled and bore a few stains.

"Good afternoon sir," Taggart grunted. "What do you want to do today?"

"Never mind that. There's a meeting at nine tomorrow you have to attend regarding the new Piano project, it's with the rest of the board members."

"I didn't know that was our project," remarked Taggart.

"It is from now on," answered the president smartly.

"Where's the meeting held?" asked Taggart of the president's instructions.

"Um.. the board room I assume. I forgot to say. Make sure the others know it's at the board room will you, thanks." Taggart's office was filled with grand bookshelves, he kept his library in his office. Papers were scattered all over the floor, some were very relevant to legal procedures he was involved in.

"You should read all the project update memos before tomorrow, Kal-El has copies if you don't. It's not that big a deal, if the board just concentrates on it for a while, as I want you to, it'll definitely get done by the end of the month. It has to be done by then, understand? Any concerns you have from now on you direct to the vice presidents and not me. There just needs to be some decision makers at the meetings in order to get something done, alright? That's you," said the president a little tired of repeating himself that afternoon. Taggart had wandered over to his coffee machine to pour himself a cup, his office smelled slightly of coffee.

"All right, is that it?" he inquired with a quiet sigh.

"Yes it should be, just talk to the other board members before the meeting tomorrow, they should fill you in with anything I haven't mentioned, okay?" The president said, a bit chirpily.

"Mmm hmm" Taggart said loudly across the room for the microphone to pick up, as he sipped his coffee and wandered back to his brown leather chair.

"Goodbye Taggart," said the president.

"Goodbye," said Taggart. The phone clicked and Taggart pressed a few buttons quickly. After thinking briefly about work he groaned and rose once more from his chair and passed his secretary's office, where he had slept on the couch the past few nights. He had sent his secretary home days ago. He kicked a nearby slipper. He went to Kal-El's office.

"The Piano memos you want are over there," Queenie said, pointing to a small pile of paper. Taggart picked some up.

"The meeting's to be in the boardroom, yes?" Taggart said to a suddenly fazed Queenie.

"I don't know," she replied. "Kal-El-" she began to call.

"No, I mean, it is in the boardroom. I'm supposed to let everyone know," Taggart corrected.

"Oh," said Queenie.

"What?" Kal-El called out. He poked his head into the room.

"The new Piano project meeting we have at nine tomorrow is in the boardroom," Taggart told Kal-El.

"Right, of course," Kal-El replied. Kal-El stood there for a moment, until he saw Taggart thank Queenie for the memos and leave, after that he returned to his office. Taggart made his way to the other offices of the board members of executive directors to tell them about the next day's meeting place. At Rahel's office they discussed the presumable absence of Sabra at the meeting. At the offices of Jacobo and Oakley, Taggart brought up this subject as well as providing the meeting venue information. On his way back to his own office he took the last sip from his coffee cup before promptly refilling it on his arrival. He glanced around his office at the mess on the floor, he thought about his divorce and his related legal trouble and groaned again, the time was two twenty-seven.

At ten twenty-four in the evening, in the same time zone as the majority of the Yellow Orang-Utan Industries board members, Gertrude removed her mouth from Mumford's ejaculating penis and went to her bathroom to rinse her mouth. Mumford followed her in minutes later where he kissed and embraced her again. After a final sexual congress that evening, Gertrude began to look forward to the next day, confident in the plans she had for it. She happily fell asleep at twelve minutes past twelve and forty-two seconds, with a pleasant wobbly feeling amongst her belly and thighs.

8.

There was a disconcerting increase in the appearance of multiple answers, with candidates apparently unsure of the correct answer.

At nine O' seven in the morning Oakley, Rahel, Jacobo, and Kal-El sat in the boardroom of the Yellow Orang-Utan Industries building.

"So really it's just a matter of a couple of us each attending the various meetings, and seeing as we have the schedule, we just need to work out an appropriate roster," Oakley was saying.

"Mmm," agreed Kal-El.

"Does it really need to be that simplistic? I mean, we have our own respective expertise to bring to this, don't we?" Rahel added, while shiny pens tapped the boardroom table.

"That's true, but that could make it a little harder to work out and the bottom line is purely a time thing," Kal-El replied.

"I s'pose it would be quicker," Rahel conceded.

"Do we roster for just the four of us here, or do we allocate meetings for Sabra and Taggart?" asked Jacobo, a little annoyed that Taggart wasn't with them, "Sabra's back next week isn't she? Taggart's around here somewhere."

"I can take this meeting here tomorrow," said Oakley looking at the schedule, "Sabra's due back Sunday morning. It should be fine, I think Taggart's running late. We could at least schedule the two of them for next week now."

"We could schedule Taggart anywhere now and just let him know about it when this meeting's over. Send him a schedule we make for him now, or something." Kal-El said with a grin.

"Are you right for these meetings on Wednesday the eighteenth, Jay?" asked Oakley, pointing to his copy of the schedule. Jacobo looked over to where Oakley pointed.

"Yes I think so," he replied, nodding his head. Everyone at the table started to pay attention to Oakley as he organised a schedule.

"Sorry I'm late," Taggart said as he wandered into the boardroom looking very sleepy. He put down his messy folder with the memos on top he collected recently. The time was nine eighteen.

At ten O' five exactly the security door opened and the security guard let Gertrude into the information technology laboratory. She asked the guard where she could find Pepito. The security guard rolled his eyes and led Gertrude amongst the poorly lit rooms of the labs. After entering a few rooms that didn't contain Pepito, they came across one that did. It was a lab full of young people looking at screens while they designed and redesigned animation software and then used it to animate the new Piano

Smedley. Pepito sat at a desk a small distance from the others, looking at a screen with the same intent as all the younger people around him.

"Pepito?" Gertrude asked as she approached his desk.

"Yes? How can I help you? What do you want to do today?" Pepito said in a very friendly and welcoming way. "Do you like what we're doing here? We're working on some conversational noddys for the new Piano." Gertrude knew very little of what Pepito referred to. She shyly introduced herself.

"My name's Gertrude, I've been coming in here recently with all the others to look at the new Piano developments."

"Uh huh, yeah. I think I've seen you amongst the herd," Pepito said. "How can I help you?"

"I was wondering if all the same processes you're going through for the new Piano are the same for the old Piano, and if you have all the old Piano files." Pepito looked at Gertrude with a puzzled look. Gertrude had the same look gazing at Pepito.

"The processes aren't quite the same, the technology is always changing and improving and stuff, we're not working with the same software from twenty years ago we made the first Piano with. You do understand that, don't you?" asked Pepito.

"Oh yeah, I understand that," replied Gertrude. "But do you have all the old Piano files that went together to make him, and all his old interviews and stuff, stuff like that?"

"Umm, yeah. We store a lot of that stuff on drives somewhere. I'm not quite sure where that is though," replied Pepito, thinking. Getrude looked at him slightly pleadingly. Pepito picked up a phone receiver, "I'll just call someone who might know," he said. Pepito made contact with another human via the telephone on his desk and got information from them. Gertrude idly looked about the laboratory.

"Come with me, I think I know where it is now," Pepito said as he put the phone receiver down. He led Gertrude through more dimly lit rooms until they found another room, well lit by windows, with lots of cabinets and shelves with thousands of documents stored amongst them. Pepito scurried alongside a shelf spying the labelled spines of a selection of drive cases.

"Here we go," announced Pepito as he pulled a drive down from its shelf position. "All the ones along here should be Piano stuff, but ah, browse around here long enough and you'll probably find some more."

"Thank you very much," Gertrude quickly and graciously said. "You can probably look at them on that, there," Pepito indicated at a computer in the corner by a window.

"Thanks heaps," gushed Gertrude. She took the pulled drive from Pepito and looked at the computer she believed she could work.

"Okay, that's that then. You'll find your way out of here when you're done won't you?" asked Pepito, exiting the room.

"I hope so," said Gertrude with wide eyes and a grin. Pepito grinned back and disappeared from Gertrude's view. She turned and went to the computer by the window. Through it the sun shone down on her as she began to affirm her beliefs about working the computer. The time was ten nineteen and fifty seconds.

Eleven twenty-three was the time when a group of market hackers, public relations officers, their affiliates, Jacobo and Rahel were gathered together. Many people there were squabbling, however Jacobo and Rahel were listening. Jacobo failed to notice the marks on the ceiling that the Yellow Orang-Utan president noticed when he was in the same gathering space with many of the same people. Rahel didn't suggest to Biscuit, standing in a corner, they sneak out of the meeting together. After listening for a while, Rahel and Jacobo started to talk amongst themselves. They nodded and listened to the others squabbling for many seconds. Jacobo coughed with a touch of drama.

"No, you can't," he said, loud enough for all gathered there to hear. There was a pause in the communications buzzing in the room. People there spoke again at eleven thirty-nine.

At eleven minutes past twelve the president of Yellow Orang-Utan Industries sat at a table and ran a hand over his stubbly face. He had just ordered lunch and was waiting for it.

Meanwhile Gertrude remembered lunch and got up from the chair by the computer that displayed some information Gertrude was interested in.

The president had spent the morning napping and watching Telly-net. He crawled into his gel window before ordering lunch, it was very warm from the sun that day. He thought about guns and shooting things, Piano Smedley and puppies. He stuck his finger in his mouth.

Gertrude was having trouble finding an exit to the laboratory area she was inside. She was growing increasingly hungry, her tummy felt cold and empty and she kept thinking of celery.

The president went into his bathroom to urinate, while holding his penis and staring into the toilet he thought about pills. After washing his hands he looked for and found pills in the bathroom.

Gertrude followed some other people walking through a corridor in the laboratory.

Wellington watched those people and noticed Gertrude join them.

Gertrude remembered there was a dining area not far past the security door.

Starting to feel hungry, and anxious from the wait, the president looked at the pill-bottle on the table he'd brought from the bathroom and thought about stronger narcotic substances.

A security guard in the Yellow Orang-Utan Industries building smiled at the crowd of luncheoners milling by the door as a special timer changed to an exact five minute interval and he opened it. When Gertrude was taking a large juicy bite from her lunch she thought about her orgasm the night before. Eating the food she had been craving, the relief of nourishment overtook her senses until she began to think more about Piano Smedley and the task she had set for herself.

A courier with the delivery of a meat and pasta dish intended for the president of Yellow Orang-Utan Industries knocked on a door. The president, with a few pills in his mouth, went to answer the knock. The time was twelve forty-nine.

At three O'clock Sabra said: "Hello, can you hear me?"

"Yes," said, Rahel, Oakley and Kal-El.

"Uh-huh," said Taggart and Jacobo. Letitia said nothing, but she smiled having got the phone system to work.

"Okay, what's going on? What's happened so far?" came Sabra's voice from the large phone in the boardroom. Sunlight through the window reflected off Letitia's buttons.

"Things have been coming together," said Kal-El. "There wasn't any clear direction in the project and the hackers and PR people were each trying to take over."

"Uh-huh," said Sabra in her Singapore hotel room into a phone receiver.

"Uh, the project wasn't going in the right direction and was going in circles with various reviews and inquiries on behalf of the er, inappropriately interested parties," mentioned Taggart.

"It was pretty sad," Rahel added, cutting in on what was to be a larger speech from Taggart, "some of them were bringing lawyers in to protect their interests."

"They'd lost a bit of focus, and become a bit selfish," began Jacobo.

"We've been shifting the project in the directions it's supposed to take," added Kal-El.

"And we've been moving back towards the interests of Yellow Orang-Utan," finished Oakley. The board members in the boardroom looked at each other and grinned or smiled.

"Things have been running OK now?" questioned Sabra.

"Yes", Oakley put forth.

"Things have been running OK now?" Sabra repeated, not hearing Oakley.

"Yes. Can you hear alright?" Letitia said loudly looking with some concern at Jacobo who had helped her connect the phone up.

"Yes, I think so, it's a bit fuzzy," Sabra loudly said into her phone.

"Just talk a bit louder," suggested Taggart quietly.

"So how are the different elements coming together?" asked the phone.

"The personal history's still being debated and discussed," began Kal-El, "and we're pretty clear on the different directions he'll take from Piano. The animation people have been working on some interviews but the scripts have yet to be written, because the personality's still being discussed, but that should be ready within the next few days. Obviously we don't have to mention the personal history ourselves, but once we announce him they'll be looking."

"News sites have already been posting rumours of the most probable new presidents. We've thrown a few out there ourselves, but we're dangling a bit, dangerously long," Taggart added.

"And we haven't had a new official name to throw out, Sabra?" teased Letitia.

"I suppose there'll be updates in the internal Yellow Orang-Utan software?" asked Sabra, before putting down the receiver to run into her hotel bathroom and throw up.

"Yes, that's not too central a concern, our focus is on the public face outside the organisation. It will happen though," replied Rahel. For a few minutes the board members looked at the quiet speaker-phone. They called out Sabra's name a bit and Letitia went pale thinking her phone connecting skills had come to nought.

"Okay, I've thought about a name for the past night or two," claimed Sabra, finally. The faces in the boardroom turned eagerly to the phone, gleams in their eyes and pens in their hands. Letitia Bjorksdottir exhaled.

"I quite liked: Vail Shamrock" came Sabra's first offer. The Yellow Orang-Utan Industries executive board members quickly scribbled the name down with various spellings.

"Uh-huh, any others?" asked Oakley politely.

"Well looking at my list, there's Wadsworth Perry, Xenos Tao, Yehudi Matembah, Zabdiel Seinfeld, and Adar Gormley," called Sabra. Rahel had been giggling at a few names.

"That's quite a list, you've certainly given us lots of interesting names to discuss, Sabra," Rahel said as she calmed down.

"Yeah, they're good Sab," offered Jacobo, loudly, remembering Taggart's suggestion.

"Where d'ya go before, Sab? We thought we'd lost you," Taggart cheerfully enquired.

"Did I cut out before? Did you hear everything properly?" asked the voice from the phone that sounded like Sabra in Singapore. She was talking around her vomiting, not wanting to mention it to the entire board.

"No, before the names," mentioned Letitia to the machine. Jacobo glanced at his watch.

"Um, I'm not sure what you mean,' Sabra said into her receiver with some nervous diplomacy.

"Things seem OK now though, those are good names Sab. We'll discuss our final choice and expect you back here next week. You'll be here when we have the launch." Oakley said, interrupting the awkwardness.

"OK," said Sabra, grinning on her bed, her breath still smelling of vomit. The time was three thirty-four.

At five forty-four that afternoon Gertrude made her way out

of the room where she had been studying the old memory drives all day. Earlier she had sat in her chair on the other side of the room from the computer that read the drives. She looked at the screen across the room and her head buzzed with quiet excitement. The sun shone through the windows and on to her warm shoulders. Gertrude's head still buzzed and she still felt warm all over as she made her way through the increasingly familiar corridors and darkness.

Then she saw Wellington enter the corridor ahead of her. Her train of thought froze and she locked her concentration on the man before her. The warmth changed in her body. She glared at the back of his head as he perambulated his way amongst the laboratory. Gertrude was carefully quiet and stealthy. Wellington unknowingly led her through a patch of laboratory turf she had yet to visit. He disappeared through a doorway which contained a door that, when Gertrude got near, turned out to be locked from the inside. TV sounds muffled their way through the door which heightened Gertrude's curiosity. She tried listening for a while, but she couldn't make out any particular voice or familiar program. She paced outside the door weighing up options, turned to go, then the door swung open and Wellington poked his head outside.

"Hallo Gertrude, I thought I heard someone outside," Wellington said with a smile.

"Don't you work in market hacking?" Gertrude snapped quickly. She peered inside a little obviously. She could see bright lights from what seemed to be many Telly-net monitors and a few computers too.

"Aren't you the PA to the president?" Wellington replied.

"I'm working on a special project concerning Piano Smedley," Gertrude told him. She looked into Wellington's dull eyes.

"Hmm, well the project I'm working on in this laboratory I can't talk about without permission from my superiors," said Wellington. Gertrude folded her arms and walked away from him and his unsatisfactory answer. Her handbag dangled and bumped against her leg rhythmically as she walked.

"Goodbye Gertrude," called Wellington warmly through the hall.

On her way out of the lab she saw two young people chatting in the corridors. As the security guard ushered her through the door at an exact time, there was nobody else exiting with her. Many inside the lab would be working late to have the necessary preparations for the launch of the new fake president of Yellow Orang-Utan Industries. Gertrude hurriedly purchased a juicy drink from the nearby lunch bar vendor and mentally cursed Wellington while the curious part of her mind mutated and evolved. After the first few mouthfuls she started to exit the Yellow Orang-Utan building. Then she quickly hoped she had her mobile phone with her at thirteen past six and twenty seconds.

At ten thirty-seven Biscuit, Mumford, Prudence and Gertrude exited a cinema talking and laughing. Biscuit laughed especially hard, much to the amusement of others. They continued walking until they found a café they wanted to visit and continued their chatter in seats. Mumford asked to be excused and went to the toilet. Another joke was cracked while he was away from their table. In the toilet Mumford decided he was bored and wanted to go home. Out the toilet Gertrude was very pleased that Prudence and Biscuit were getting along. Mumford returned to the table and announced his boredom and intention to go home. Gertrude walked with him to the street before saying goodbye. Meanwhile Prudence told Biscuit a good story about some of her experiences earlier that year, Biscuit listened politely and intently and with a hint of glee. Gertrude returned to the table when both the other women had finished their warm drinks. The time was eleven eighteen at night.

At eleven O' clock that night the president spent five minutes telling his desk about how much he would enjoy a massage at this time. He did not realise it was his desk he spoke to. He had not shaved for days. His sheet smelled, his body was brewing with chemicals and genetically engineered food. Eventually he passed out at two past midnight.

9.

How clean a car would you buy if its exhaust pipe, instead of being aimed at pedestrians, fed directly into the passenger compartment?

- Natural Capitalism, 1999

At twelve thirty exactly Gertrude exited the tech-lab and went to the nearby lunch kiosk. She bought some yoghurt and fruit and began to spoon it in her mouth with a bad attitude. She partly blamed the buzz – the pressure surrounding the announcement of the new Piano. It seemed to surround her too, it was tonight. Here in the lunch kiosk, the faces around her looked very stressed as they shovelled nourishment into their mouths. Tonight's announcement meant they were all working extra hard for the media events that would ensue. There was a lot of litter on the tables around her, many lab employees had been keeping irregular hours, hours that didn't accommodate the cleaner's schedule well. At twelve fifty-one, she quietly groaned in frustration.

At one seventeen a glass with sparkling wine in it was tapped repeatedly with cutlery to gain attention from the market hackers, public relations officers, the vice presidents and board of executive directors of

Yellow Orang-Utan Industries gathered in the large function room. There were a lot of others gathered in the room too, but why they were there was uncertain to most attending, some of themselves included. Letitia beamed like a proud parent while younger people who didn't realise her position in the corporation talked to her excitedly. Kal-El had decided to give an impromptu speech, perhaps because he'd too much alcohol. Those gathered close to Kal-El listened politely, those not gathered close continued talking together, although more discreetly.

The new Piano project had neared its completion. It was the end of the month and there was appropriate cause for celebration. The tables in the function room were lined with plates of expertly prepared food for all assembled to devour. There was more than just Kal-El's glass containing sparkling wine. There was more than just sparkling wine to drink. With the project over the market hackers and public relations officers were relieved they were no longer obligated to get along any more. Consequently, the two groups were getting along better than ever.

The board of directors were especially pleased this novel assignment had reached fruition. Oakley was currently on his phone talking to his wife, he had previously been talking to his daughter. He was very happy and wanted to make incredible plans for his weekend with them. Kal-El was merrily drunk and making a good speech. Rahel and Sabra whispered together.

"Have you decided what you are to do?" Rahel asked discreetly.

"Yes," answered Sabra with a big grin, whisper-quiet.

"Well?" asked Rahel, barely whisper-quiet.

"I decided in Singapore, I'm going to keep it" Sabra declared, especially quietly. Rahel squealed in delight. People watching the speech looked at her and she apologised quietly to them.

"It's a bit too late to change my mind anyway," continued Sabra while Rahel told her how happy she was for her. Taggart felt good from the recommended pills, from the recommended therapist, from his recommended lawyer. He smiled cheerfully and rocked gently on his feet. Jacobo cheekily flirted with an employee he had not met before. Kal-El attempted to extend thanks and congratulations to whatever people whose name he could remember, then he raised his glass a little higher to finish off.

"To Zabdiel Seinfeld," he said loud enough for everyone to hear. Many people assembled hadn't heard the name before, then it dawned on them who the middle aged drunk man in the loose brown shirt and beads was referring to. Many began to clap as those knowing he shouldn't have mentioned the name made eye contact with each other across the room with disapproving looks on their faces. Palmira cackled with laughter.

"Sssh," hushed Oakley standing nearby, a grin appearing on his face. Queenie chortled with the little air she had while trying to contain a large mouthful of chocolate cake. A young man facing her turned towards Kal-El and inquired as to what he said to no one in particular. Someone dropped a cheap and disposable plate. Karel chewed slowly, feeling mildly disinterested. A few public relations people grabbed their phones to inform associates in the news reporting profession of the identity of the new Yellow Orang-Utan president, dialling as fast as their little fingers would allow. The hubbub of conversation returned to the room in the familiar party pattern. Letitia stood with her hands on her hips, looking rather cross. She wondered where Naamah Nelise, the other vice president of Yellow Orang-Utan Industries had got to. The time was twenty to two.

At ten to two, the president of Yellow Orang-Utan Industries was running through murky corridors shooting people's heads off with the explosive force that only state of the art automatic weapons could offer. At least he thought he was doing that. He was actually sitting on his bed twiddling buttons on a control pad for a three dimensional digital environment game that displayed the actions of a lead character from the position of the point of view of that fictional character. The Wall-span TV displayed a two dimensional simulation of that game that the president stared at intently. Then an item popped up on the screen indicating some special internal e-mail had reached the president. He was a little upset to receive it when he had requested no such thing but paused his game and went to his desk to see what it was.

When he saw what it was he thought for a moment about how long he had not been paying attention to the corporation he had founded in his youth. The corporation that had become the most powerful in the world. Then he double-checked the screen for the name Zabdiel Seinfeld. There were lots of e-mails from the past few weeks that he had deleted before reading the latest one. He wondered if something was amiss. Then he decided the drugs were just making him paranoid. He went to the bathroom and washed his face before returning to his bed. He un-paused his video game and resumed play. He wanted to finish this game very much, he wanted to explode into liquid goop all kinds of gargantuan monsters with his big gun. The time was two fifty-nine.

At three past four Gertrude had decided enough was enough for what would not be the only time and knocked on the door to Wellington's secretive room. She quickly pictured cactus in her mind as she waited for a response, there wasn't any. She felt stupid waiting for too long a time (five minutes and thirteen seconds) and walked away to the room she had habitually visited for too many days. She thought about ways to cool off her frustration. The time was thirteen past four and twenty seconds when Gertrude began an exhalation of breath.

At three minutes past six Wellington strode the corridors of the information technology laboratory of the Yellow Orang-Utan Industries building. He was going to the room he often had to himself there. On his way he spotted three giggling workers whose names he knew sitting on discarded orthopaedic chairs. He did not ponder what he would behold in his room at all. Further on his way Gertrude nearly walked into him, her face displaying a look of someone lost in thought. She looked at him with surprise very quickly, her eyebrows raised on her expertly sculpted face before changing her look to something different to surprise.

"I want to know-" she rapidly began before pausing and breathing. Wellington looked at her with an inviting face indicating the appreciation he'd have for her to finish what she was saying. He had no chance to say hello.

"-What you're up to in that room," finished Gertrude.

"The room you saw me in most recently?" asked Wellington. Gertrude looked into Wellington's eyes with a very determined look in hers.

"Yes," she replied.

"As you know, I'm not to say without permission. But I suspect you'd like me to get permission," he said, opening an offer. Gertrude looked at him quizzically after he spoke.

"Yes, very much," she responded, a perturbed curiosity lacing her voice.

"I will get permission Gertrude, and I will then find you and grant you your wish, if you really wish to know." Wellington said with a restrained smile so as not to appear too condescending.

"Yeah, I would," claimed Gertrude slapping her clipboard to her side.

"Very well, I will contact you very soon after I have permission from my superiors Gertrude, good evening." Wellington walked past Gertrude and continued on his way. Wellington came to the door of the fading secret that was his room and neatly swiped a security card through the appropriate slot. A little light went green at six thirteen and forty seconds as Wellington pushed the door open.

Mumford was grinning his perverse grin as Gertrude entered her home at forty-five minutes past six O' clock in the evening.

"Howdy," he said sleepily. Gertrude offered him a similar greeting. He leapt up and hugged her and they swayed there on her lounge room floor for a while.

"You smell weird ever since you've been going to that computer lab every day," he announced with a muffled chuckle. Gertrude groaned and smiled at the same time before she replied.

"Well I'm nearly finished there." Gertrude's television was on and the Telly-net sound bytes burped from the corner, distracting the huggers. They told the story of the officially announced new president of Yellow Orang-Utan. Gertrude sat down on her couch and watched more carefully the reports that displayed the faces of Zabdiel Seinfeld and Piano Smedley.

She picked things out that Mumford couldn't discern from the reports. Neither, however, paid attention to the heavily sculpted news anchor's mentioning that the time of the announcement was made early that afternoon. Wellington had, but that was yet to be any business of Gertrude's. As the news stories wafted away from stories that interested Mumford, he went into another room and returned to sit on the couch with an object in his possession. Gertrude and Mumford continued to stare at the television screen watching the images that still entertained them without interesting stories. Until Mumford spoke softly to Gertrude and showed her what he had brought from her bedroom.

Gertrude instantly guffawed at the blow-up Piano Smedley sexual aid, but then she stopped as she guessed Mumford's intentions for it. Mumford's eyes danced with excitement in his proud face, he grinned on the point of drooling.

"Will you try it out with me?" he asked playfully.

"I don't think so," asserted Gertrude. Mumford continued trying to convince her, and she playfully rejected each consecutive offer. He reacted with small pouts before he eventually gave up halfway through their dinner. As Gertrude tidied her kitchen after their cooking and eating, Mumford made a phone call. It began to ring at seven minutes to eight O' clock.

At ten past nine at night the president paused his game to massage his sore thumbs and fingers. He rolled backwards on to his bed and became lost in laconic thinking. The Wall-span TV buzzed with electricity. He had visited a news site a few times since the afternoon's e-mail, for updates, but not much had happened. He sat back up and checked it again to see experts discuss important matters of finance and politics, a few names he knew were mentioned. Yellow Orang-Utan Industries was possibly mentioned too, but he couldn't pay enough attention to be sure.

He visited some of the more popular media portholes on Telly-net. He surfed through more news, contemporary drama and comedy, music television and feature films. He used tools to narrow his searching, and then surfed some more. He saw a comedian commenting upon contemporary issues, already ridiculing Zabdiel Seinfeld and Yellow Orang-Utan. It was the last thing the president saw before he reached the phone to order dinner. He ordered more narcotics with the side dish of fast food he'd been consuming lately, again without questioning their effects on the various interconnected aspects of his health. The Telly-net sound bytes left no impression on him as he commanded Windle through a telephone line. As the order was prepared for human safety and mechanical transport, the president resumed his game with eagerness. A well-endowed female cyborg crashed against a wall leaving a green bloody smear at fourteen past ten.

The moments after Gertrude put down the phone receiver felt unreal. The time was twenty-four minutes and twenty three-seconds before eleven O' clock. She was rearranging her clothes for bed, then she was brushing her teeth. Wellington had rung earlier that evening, just after dinner.

"I have something to tell you, Gertrude," he had begun. After, of course letting her know it was he who spoke from the phone.

"How did you get my number?" Gertrude had asked, feeling slightly intruded and wanting to know. Wellington temporarily abandoned his information supply to explain.

"It's available on databases at Yellow Orang-Utan Industries, Gertrude," Wellington said.

"I have permission to tell you about the room, if you'd like to hear it," he continued.

"Go on," she egged.

"But-"

"But what?"

"There's something else, something primarily more important, that I can also tell you," said a little speaker inside Gertrude's phone receiver.

"What is it?"

"I am a robot." Gertrude thought this such a strange thing to claim she snapped a curse reply.

"I assure you it's true," continued Wellington, "my superiors and I would like to ask for a meeting with you tomorrow to explain things more thoroughly in person. Can you meet me in the room you've been asking about? At about eight O' clock tomorrow morning?" Gertrude paused, she felt lied to.

"Yes," she eventually answered.

"I can explain about the room then, if you'd like. But I can do it no-"

"Wellington," interrupted Gertrude.

"Yes?" Wellington asked, patiently.

"What do you use your black card for?"

"I haven't," began Wellington, but he paused.

"My superiors and I would prefer to discuss this all tomorrow," he finished.

"Uh-huh, see you then," said Gertrude, scowling.

"Good bye," Wellington had said.

The conversation burned in Gertrude's memory as she rearranged her clothes for bed and then brushed her teeth. She felt very patronised to be lied to like that, but while her head rested on her pillow she wondered at the sense it made, the possibility it could be true. Mumford had his warm hands inside her loose clothing, as he kissed her she gave her attention to him. His mouth moved over her body in a way she was now familiar with. When he thought she was ready, their embrace shifted to another comfortable position, he pleaded once more to use the Piano Smedley inflatable sex doll in their remaining conscious hours.

"No," she said, rather irritated. She sucked on his neck when she decided enough was enough again. At seventeen minutes past eleven, their pelvic tissues voluntarily ground against each other in a room absent of physical representations of Piano Smedley.

10.

Deep down, past all the sexism, racism, anger and self-loathing, he's a sensitive, compassionate new-age guy.

At four O' clock the following morning Mumford and Gertrude were not unconscious. Gertrude told Mumford rather grumpily to go sleep on the couch. Mumford slowly made his confused and angered way to the couch where he tried to sleep. Gertrude rolled over in her bed, she got lost between falling back to sleep and, enough being enough, mentally preparing herself. Before her clock sounded an alarm, she went to him half asleep and half-dressed. Mumford watched a length of her hair fall as she told him it was over.

As she prepared for her meeting with Wellington and his superiors, Mumford tried to argue with her. There were raised voices, and excreted tears that were quickly wiped. The argument degraded to whom used who for sex as Gertrude pulled on her shoe.

"Don't be here when I get back," Gertrude said sternly.

"Okay," replied Mumford quietly, hugging a couch cushion, bedding draped around his half naked form.

Gertrude left her home. While waiting at the station she discreetly painted her face with her preferred glossed-flesh taint. She entered an accommodating vehicle that she was confident would take her to an appropriate walking distance to the Yellow Orang-Utan Industries building. During her journey she piped music inside her head with a small media player. It was often a mild distraction from the traffic and the fellow travellers around her.

She walked into the ground floor of the Yellow Orang-Utan building and past an expansive reception foyer. Entering an elevator, she breathed deeply. When she left the elevator, Gertrude walked down a hallway that would lead to the information technology laboratory, past a row of vending machines that sold the juicy frozen popsicles that shone like chrome all the way to the stick. At the entrance to the laboratory, there was a tired and amicable security guard waiting at the door to open it for Gertrude. At an exact time it opened and she walked through the doorway. As Gertrude wended her way through the dark corridors she became incensed with specific nervous curiosity. She knocked on a particular door. A little green light went on and a familiar face appeared from behind the slightly ajar door.

"Hi Gertrude, please come in," said Pepito with a slight sigh. Gertrude followed the middle-aged man into the room where she saw Wellington with his large fuzz of hair. He wore baggy pants and she wore a neat and simple yellow shirt under a dull, businesslike jacket.

"Hallo Gertrude," Wellington said.

"Would you like some coffee?" asked Pepito, indicating two cups on a chair. Gertrude thought about the coffee before agreeing and taking some.

"Is anybody else coming?" she asked after her first sip on the warm sugary drink.

"No there's just me, I'm in charge of Wellington. I made him, he's a robot," answered Pepito after his first sip. Gertrude sat on the wooden chair that the coffees had rested on. Behind Wellington was a bunch of Telly-net monitors built into the wall, they were off. Behind Gertrude were a bunch of computer engines in their cases that whirred with activity. They sat in rows on a table that was just as the other tables in the lab were. Pepito sat on the edge of a chair beside the table, his leg tapped rapidly.

"That's correct, Gertrude," offered Wellington earnestly. Gertrude looked into a robot's face for a while.

"Does he work in market hacking?" Gertrude asked Pepito, craning her neck back to face him.

"Mmm hmm, I got him a job there. He practised here in this room and he managed some virtual shares. His work was really remarkable, he worked for me and he boosted my superannuation...heaps." Pepito said, with a noisy slurp on his coffee, "we wondered if we could run him alongside the proper guys in the company, so I installed him in the employee database as a market hacker. He's got a workstation with them now and that's his uh, his day job." Pepito was keen to spill his guts about the robot he was very proud to have built, but instead he just sat there while Gertrude stared pensively at Wellington's amicable face.

"He checks in here every night because he gets a build up of memory every day. He works like a lot of robots you've probably seen on Telly-net. A lot of his day-to-day interactions are automatic. Kind of like Piano and Zabdiel, the way they work in interviews, but we write the dialogue for those guys whereas Wellington manufactures his own. But I've equipped him with all the top of the line reading software I can get my hands on, including psychological reading stuff like the on-line psychic avatars." Pepito volunteered, breaking a long silence.
"The what?" asked Gertrude.

"The on-line psychics, you send them ah, your complaint, with pictures and video and such and they interpret it and give you a 'psychic' reading. There's one or two that act as more serious therapists too. The real, human therapists have sued them too, 'cause they have proved to be effective with their patients, and the human therapists lose business. But they're just reading the signs and symbols people give out in their body language and face expressions and stuff, and measuring that up with the stories people tell them. It's kind of, ah, measured and automatic but it comes off as pretty intuitive too, and Wellington works like that. When you talk to him he'll make a psychological profile of you and be basing his interaction on that. Then he comes back here and unloads the data he builds up. All the interactions and conversations he has, he records. He unloads them on to these computers behind you and we run them through all the reading software-"

"We compare the readings from the various programs and make a hybrid interpretation, which analyses the memory files we have of the people I interact with," interrupted Wellington. "The software I use in my day to day interaction with everybody is a program of Pepi's and my own design, based on the other reading programs we acquired from other authors. I've been incorporating many other theoretical bases for interpreting people outside of the Freudian, Jung-Campbell and neo Spock bases typical of the average psychological reading software, including theories that aren't even particularly of a psychological nature." Gertrude stared at the robot, slightly confused.

"Woah," she sighed, a little taken back by the jargon. Pepito looked over Gertrude's head at Wellington proudly.

"But we were worried this might make him a bit too perfect, or ah, he might know too much about the people he talks too. With psychological profiles, he might know more about the person than they have realised about themselves, perhaps? So what I've set up on his memory bank computers behind you is a little program that randomly erases some of the files, so when he goes to interact with people, he might forget some of the details about them," Pepito said, before Wellington piped in again.

"But my automatic responses compensate a bit and don't make me seem rude or stupid," piped Wellington. Gertrude shifted her chair to glance more easily at the two characters spouting information at her, she was pursing her lips and scowling quite a bit as she reacted to the things they were saying.

"What about the black card?" she asked, never being one to think highly of holders of such cards. Pepito let a small laugh out of his mouth.

"I've never used the black card, Gertrude," assured Wellington. "The fundamental aspects of my programming stop me from ever breaking laws, as well as special laws Pepi installed especially for robots. But the black card that gets you off for breaking the law merely gives the impression that there's a chance I might break the law. I decided it would put me, symbolically, on par with everybody else, who have the real sentience allowing them to break laws, otherwise-"

"We can steal candy, and we can think about stealing candy. But Wellington can't steal candy, but with the black card he can at least think about it. He won't, but he can entertain the idea of theft, which expands his thinking potential, some scenarios he can't understand without the card," offered an interrupting Pepito, thinking highly of his candy example.

"Uh huh," Gertrude muttered compliantly.

"In any case, Wellington has never been out of this building to have done anything illegal," Pepito added. Gertrude looked at Wellington and gave a small expression of surprise. Pepito took another mouthful of coffee or two. Gertrude had abandoned hers, as she didn't like its taste too much, she sat upon her chair with arms folded.

"What about walking around and stuff? He looks real," Gertrude demanded, turning to Pepito.

"Well, that part's easy, it's been done before by other people. There are working androids out there that look real and get about easily and look very comfortable doing it," claimed Pepito, "I think Wellington's a bit different because most robots aren't as effective talking to people. People pick them out, but I think it's because they aren't developing them with psyche-reading software as much as I have with Wellington, they're normally just programmed with automated responses and mimicking software. Wellington has mimicking software too, 'cause it can fool a lot of people as some of the other robots I've seen have."

"You're the only person who has had the suspicion that I am not similar to themselves, that is, human," Wellington said suddenly. The two humans in the room looked at the robot. Gertrude kept looking while Pepito looked at his wristwatch.

"We were wondering if you would take him out with you sometimes, to see how he does outside of the building," Pepito mentioned reluctantly, unsure how big a favour he was asking of Gertrude. Gertrude looked at the pair of them with some concern.

"Why can't you do it Pepi?"

"Because I have a job to do, and I can't babysit my robot all the time, and I need to sleep and eat," Pepito replied humorously. The information about Wellington was too new for Gertrude to be sure what to do.

"Do you mean like, a romantic date going out thing, or what?" she asked.

"Oh, no, no, not anything like that, just take him out to a social sort of atmosphere, test him on your friends, that sort of thing." Gertrude sat there for a while with a firm jaw and a furrowed brow, thinking.

"Why did you make a robot at all?" she asked Pepito.

"I was curious about it, and now that I've done it, I want to see what I can do with him. I've already done quite a bit, he's a good market hacker who's fooled everyone in that part of the building," answered Pepito precisely. Gertrude exhaled before making an admission.

"I'll think about it," she admitted. It would require a lot of thinking, she thought then to herself. The two male resembling figures in the room thanked her with various levels of apparent sincerity. They continued to discuss some jargon heavy matters as Gertrude left the room feeling strange, she took a minute to compose herself and then proceeded to the familiar small library she'd been studying in at eight thirty-six.

At a quarter past ten the president of Yellow Orang-Utan Industries pressed his control pad button very excitedly. His face expressed his emotions dramatically, he stared at the screen with big wide eyes. He was nearly finished his computer game! Every attempt to complete the final stage became increasingly urgent, he was learning the pattern of the computer's simulated attack on his controllable character. The president was very excited as he anticipated the inspirational concluding sequence that would begin when he completed the final necessary task. There was a gory explosion on screen and the president cooed in appreciation and victory. The time was now ten-twenty one.

Mumford was rather upset and angry at eleven minutes past eleven. He sat on a chair in Gertrude's rather messy lounge room and stared blankly into space wallowing in thought. He looked at the Piano Smedley inflatable sexual aide in its packaging on the chair beside him. He sunk back into the cushioning of his chair and exhaled moodily.

He reached over for the aide while rubbing his crotch. He placed the packaging on his lap and looked at the labelling of it. Some of it was mis-spelled, Mumford guessed, but couldn't be sure because his spelling knowledge wasn't that good and a dictionary wasn't anywhere in sight. Still rubbing his groin, Mumford rummaged amongst the ordinary objects on Gertrude's coffee table for her television's remote control. He found it and switched it on and pressed buttons until he found an appropriately pornographic Telly-net site. The site signalled a sexual performance that pleased him. As his erection developed, Mumford pulled the Piano Smedley sex aide out of its package and fiddled with it until it began to quickly inflate. Piano Smedley's form oddly materialised before the aroused man.

He held the light doll in his arms and placed its plastic erection in his mouth. The doll's voice synthesiser cried out in response. He cast it aside while he quickly and ungracefully struggled out the few clothes he had on. Mumford then bent Piano down and played with Smedley like a puppet. Its face of unvarying skin tone worked its way up Mumford's expertly crafted thigh implants. Mumford had it kissing his legs and then performing fellatio upon his erect penis. He sat back and watched the pornography on Gertrude's television until he felt chafed by the plastic inflation making friction on the skin surrounding his genitals.

The sound, synchronised with the streaming video from the Telly-net, declared in human voices that people were feeling very good and then proceeded to call each other names in between squeals and moans. Mumford threw the Piano Smedley inflatable sexual aide on a nearby lounge. He tried to masturbate to the musical language of Telly-net porn briefly before leaping upon his recent purchase and wedging his penis inside the fake plastic anus of Piano Smedley. The doll's voice synthesiser shrieked in pleasure. The audio-visual porn droned on while the Piano Smedley voice synthesiser continued to communicate in a similar language.

Mumford mentally braced himself for an orgasm he wanted to have as his manicured pelvis jostled with a synthetic bottom. Despite his implants' surgical manipulation, Mumford's natural flesh buttocks began to feel cold. He looked at the back of the Piano Smedley sex doll's head and neck. The cheap voice synthesiser began to sound pathetic. He looked at his extended penis shafted inside the cleverly marketed Yellow Orang-Utan merchandise. He pulled out, abandoning his idea of ever using the sexual device again, and completed his task in Gertrude's bathroom. The image of a young woman's heavily painted, semen ridden face licking a well built man's waxed sphincter on a television screen faded to black at eleven thirty-four.

The president happily munched on a lettuce leaf at twelve forty-one. After completing his video game, he had dressed and arranged a healthy salad for his lunch. It had been a while since he even ate salad at all. The president ate his lunch at a desk in a room he'd often worked in before. The lettuce and other vegetables glistened with a tasty oily dressing, the light blue ruffles of his lettuce disappeared inside his mouth with a related oily slurp. Lunch was quite nice, but he had a bad headache, from the combination of noisy video games and his continued abuse of pharmaceuticals. He felt yucky and decided he would have a shower after lunch, then began to plan what to do after that.

A small screen at the desk displayed news headlines and related video. The president looked at the screen occasionally while thinking about chefs and changing musical technology. Soon he decided he would watch as many of the *Greenacres* episodes as he could before he got tired or hungry or both. As he finished his salad he peered into the bottom of his lunch bowl and tried to gather as much of the small bits of food on to his fork as they bobbed and swayed in the blue puddle of salad dressing. The time was three past one.

Amongst the offices of the executive board members at Yellow Orang-Utan Industries there were more than one face displaying stress and concern at one twelve. Many of them watched the same or similar news that the president had been watching while he ate lunch. Their mental grasp of the day's news was much greater than the president's. Jacobo and Rahel read screens. Sabra read printed reports, and feared during her morning that her legs were getting fatter and would need implanting. Taggart and Oakley listened to people they talked to on their telephones. Kal-El was in a meeting with Naamah Nelise, a vice president of Yellow Orang-Utan Industries. Later he would write things at a rather furious speed. They were asking questions, occasionally Oakley, Kal-El or Taggart would get answers, their technology use being a little more interactive. Sabra, Jacobo and Rahel would merely ask the questions in their minds, their eyebrows furrowed so to crease their foreheads. Taggart was now officially divorced and developing a reliance on rather expensive emotional painkillers. Some of their thoughts during the day they feared being paranoia. The minuscule mental seed of suspicion had been planted in their minds firmly and would grow for the remainder of the afternoon. Grow well up to the time when they each received the memo from Zabdiel Seinfeld, the president of Yellow Orang-Utan Industries, at three thirty-seven.

Gertrude exhaled at three twenty-four that afternoon towards her screen and looked at the Piano files that remained to be read. There weren't many and she was determined to finish, today. She shifted in her chair, thinking about tasks to be performed the next week. She decided to stay here as late as she needed to get through all the files. Her decision was somewhat motivated by the fear she'd find Mumford still at her house when she left the Yellow Orang-Utan building. She had already received a message from an acquaintance regarding the break up. Gertrude had been hoping to get drunk, or high, with her friends that post break up evening, but it would have to wait until she was through with these files. Unfortunately, she imagined this meant not leaving until dark, uncertain of the exact time. The time then was three thirty-two.

Five minutes later at three thirty-seven, a memo from Zabdiel Seinfeld, the president of Yellow Orang-Utan was issued to the offices of all who bore them in the Yellow Orang-Utan building, the first of its kind ever. Zabdiel warmly introduced himself to the staff at Yellow Orang-Utan and explained his happiness to be the new head of their company. The public relations officers gasped when beholding the message, one even clapping facetiously, which made a secretary giggle. Zabdiel assured them of his skills as leader by briefly alluding to his past while market hackers receiving his assurances sneered a little and the animators grinned. His hopes were very sincere, to do as good a job as Piano Smedley and some other fellow whose name was lost on many. Later other messages of introduction would be seen by subsidiary companies of Yellow Orang-Utan and clients and investors and associates throughout the world. Some would be on the news. Soon other such messages from Zabdiel Seinfeld would issue forth throughout the building, sometimes a blanket message for everyone, sometimes messages for individual staff members or floors or committees. Yet it seemed strange to many reading the message it was still only three thirty-seven.

One president of Yellow Orang-Utan Industries did not receive another message from another president of Yellow Orang-Utan Industries that day and was watching *Greenacres* on the Telly-net at eight minutes past eight in the evening. He'd already eaten his dinner of sugary food but rather than the pills that had become a standard after-dinner treat of late, the president was drinking alcohol. It was hard and heavy liquor, but well disguised under a pleasant and syrupy mixer. The president was drunk while he checked how many episodes of *Greenacres* he had yet to watch. He sat in his bed, smelly and dishevelled, surrounded by his familiar satin sheets, with the addition of several stains he'd deposited on them recently. He sat on his bed occasionally laughing out loud at something he saw on the giant screen while drinking away his ability to see the giant screen at all clearly.

There was a connection between *Greenacres* and Yellow Orang-Utan Industries. That the secret president of the world's biggest corporation was a fan was part of it, but another part revealed itself to the president while he drank and laughed. Whether or not Yellow Orang-Utan Industries owned the rights to distribute episodes of *Greenacres* over the Telly-net, and owned a lot more other shows that were likely lumped together as a package, a library of TV, the president was not sure of. It could be that a business agreement between different owners and Yellow

Orang-Utan Industries had been made, perhaps some kind of licensing deal to produce what was advertised to the president while he watched episodes of *Greenacres*, or perhaps advertising through this site was merely for sale to anyone including the producers of what was advertised. And the producers were definitely connected to Yellow Orang-Utan Industries in some way because what was advertised to the president was the Piano Smedley biographic film, now complete and available to view by following a link.

The president made a mental note of the movie availability and took another sip of his drink. A few episodes of *Greenacres* later, even though mind numb and eyes tired from staring at the shimmering wall for hours, the biological form of the president of Yellow Orang-Utan switched to the site that had the Piano Smedley biographical film. It was rather useless now, everything was doubling before his eyes, but with the determination of an old man possessed by intoxicants, the president persevered. As he started the movie he made out the face of a handsome young actor who he presumed would be portraying Piano Smedley. The hardest part for the president in comprehending the movie was not his sleepiness, drunkenness or attention span as much as five minutes into the film the president's eyes failed and he became blind. The former official president of Yellow Orang-Utan Industries watched the image of an actor portraying his much loved successor, Piano Smedley fade to black and it was the last thing he'd ever see with those eyes ever.

It took a while for the president to react to the organ failure. But when a loud dramatic moment of the movie aroused his attention, his eyes weren't reacting properly. He could feel his eyelids moving but the usual opening motion came without the desired stimulation of the visual receptors of his brain. When the president grasped this, a phenomenon he'd had some experience with, he shifted his position on his bed from one resembling sitting to one resembling lying down and let out a groan. Still holding the remote control, the unseen sights and pesky sounds of the TV died immediately before the president crawled across his big bed and around the nearby stretches of floor until he found a communications console. He dialled for Windle although when he got through to him the president was slightly incoherent.

"Yes mm, Windle here, who's calling?" asked Windle when the connection was made. After the president identified himself he asked things of Windle, it was Windle's job to respond and follow relevant instructions.

"Where's Gertrude, Windle?" asked the Yellow Orang-Utan president.

"Just a minute," replied Windle as he checked a monitor that screened Gertrude's whereabouts for every moment of her life.

"According to the latest records she's at a nightclub called *Fishpaste* in the city, sir," Windle forwarded.

"Could I please have a bodyguard and driver with a car waiting for me at the bottom of the building? Please Windle?" the president pleaded, excessively.

"Of course, sir," answered Windle already dutifully arranging the request with dextrous button pushing. The president thanked Windle and exchanged a few more pleasantries before terminating the call.

He had felt around for clothes and dressed himself in a robe over the pyjamas he already had on before becoming blind. He had crawled out the door to his room and was now half way down a corridor. He figured by the time he'd make it to the ground floor the bodyguard and driver would be waiting for him. It was ten minutes to eleven as he fumbled with the elevator buttons and began a rapid descent downwards from an enormous height.

It was twenty four minutes past eleven O' clock when Gertrude removed another sip of a sweet tasting beverage from her glass. It was quite a tall glass and the beverage it contained nearly gone. This was not the first of such tall glasses Gertrude had removed the contents from this evening. She was in *Fishpaste* and she was with friends so how drunk she was didn't matter. The sugar and fizz of the bright red liquid tickled her throat unpleasantly but she was at the point in the night where the taste of the drinks was not as important as their intoxicating qualities.

She looked at the blurring visions of her friends encouraging her to smile with happy conversation. Biscuit and Sensae and Prudence were significant members of her condoling party, she had separate thoughts about them while she drank. There were others there supporting her, and grateful to be so. Gertrude thought less specific thoughts about them. Earlier they had danced, but a lot of them were too tired for that now. Between trips to the bar and toilets, they talked with the skill and care required when competing with loud club music. The music that some more energetic people continued dancing to, a group gathered mostly around Ted Showbiz.

A rapidly approaching point in the night would help focus the things in her mind. The atmosphere in the club changed strangely when a small wrinkly man with horrible breath, in thin pyjamas and a robe, came crawling along the floor of the club.

"Gertrude!" the man cried. "Gertrude!" The man had arrived outside the club in an expensive vehicle and was half-carried out by a burly man towards the media-bar entrance. There was a confrontation between the burly man and the bar's security staff before the smaller man with the burly usher mysteriously produced from his bed-clothed person a very exclusive credit card that silenced both larger men and gained the smelly drunk access. Not being able to see, he fumbled and crawled his way across the dance floor. He grabbed legs occasionally and the bearers of the legs would shake off the bent figure and scurry towards the farthest wall-of-glowing-screen. The club attendees not already having their legs molested joined the scurriers, creating an empty space for the odd man crawling like a baby with an arm outstretched as if blind. Those dancing stopped even though the loud music continued to play. Those talking despite the loud music stopped too, including Gertrude whose mouth began to dry as it

74

hung open in surprise. The only voice that could be heard was calling.

"Gertrude! Gertrude!" The president of Yellow Orang-Utan Industries was sounding increasingly desperate as he neared the furthest reaches of the nightclub. Gertrude stepped forward onto the empty dance floor and waited for the drunken elderly man to find her legs. The club-goers watched excitedly, her closer friends sitting around their booth looked a bit more concerned. The *Fishpaste* regular stood there calmly.

"Yes, it's me," was Gertrude's reply to the man's umpteenth cry, as he climbed up her legs and latched on to her dress.

"Oh, oh Gertrude, thank goodness. I'm blind Gertrude, I need your help!" he wailed above the music, with a drunken slur. Gertrude bent down nearer him so she could smell the alcohol on his breath, and he, the sugar on hers.

"Get me to a hospital please, please Gertrude," he pleaded.

"Where's Windle, why hasn't he taken care of you?" asked Gertrude sensibly as the surprise encounter had her rapidly sobering.

"I don't want Windle. I want you Gertrude, I want you!" the man said, raising his voice dramatically.

"Can you take me to a hospital, can you?" he repeated. The bodyguard had made it inside the club and stood beside the couple on the empty dance floor. She held the clutching man at arms length firmly and stood up.

"It's time you returned to work for me," he said. The time was eight minutes to midnight and forty-four seconds.

11.

The presentation of scenes, episodes, plots etc., which are deliberately meant to excite these manifestations on the part of the audience is always wrong, is subversive to the interest of society, and a peril to the human race.

- The Motion Picture Production Code, 1930

Gertrude's alarm sounded at six O'clock in the morning. The previous night she walked out of *Fishpaste* with the president back to Yellow Orang-Utan Industries building and, in consultation with Windle and Dr. Westaway, seen that the old man had proper medical treatment and rest. Gertrude finally returned home to be greeted by the discarded, inflatable form of Piano Smedley in her lounge room. She immediately ignored it and dumped herself in bed the next room over, mimicking Dr. Westaway's rest instructions to the president. After sleeping the day through, confronting Mumford's farewell detritus was the next priority. In the fog of exhaustion, Gertrude found herself dialling her therapist service on her phone first, as she waited on hold, she was reminded about Wellington's discussion of digital therapist algorithms, and hung up. Locating something sufficiently sharp in her small apartment kitchen, Gertrude stabbed Piano Smedley. The audio components responded, and as it crumpled from pressure release, she removed the power source to shut it up. With more of Gertrude's kitchen resourcefulness, the inflatable doll was then confined to a bag.

Gertrude rose to her six O'clock alarm and prepared for the new day, returning to her personal assistant role with the president of Yellow orang-Utan Industries. On the way out of her building, a former corporate president, a former sexual aide, was shoved in a bin and Gertrude continued her commute. She stepped inside the train at five minutes past nine.

At nine twenty-eight in the morning Gertrude walked into the president's room where he slept in a big bed. On the other side of the room the Wall-span TV hummed incredibly quiet on stand-by.
"Good Morning sir, what would you like to do today, sir?" Gertrude said loud enough to wake her employer.

"Good morning, Gertrude," the president answered with enough deliberation to prove beyond Gertrude's doubt that he was definitely awake. With the aid of marvellous medicine they were both very alert to begin anew their daily toil.

"I really don't know Gertrude, what's on your clip-board?" was the man in the bed with fresh sheets' response to Gertrude's customary question.

"You ought to catch up on you e-mail, sir. Your organisers' been reminding us to check a lot of important reports sent there," replied the personal assistant.

"Very well, dress me for breakfast and then we'll do that," said the president, he moved to get up from his custom designed bed. He remembered pharmaceutical cleansers that were sent through his various body systems by expert medical professionals somewhere in the middle of a recent night.

"Wait, what colour are they?" the president asked of his eyes, which he was seeing through this morning. Gertrude moved away from the door and towards the president on the edge of his bed. Her eyes widened as she looked at them closely.

"Th-they're, um, the left one is brown and the right one is all milky white. I think it's discoloured," was the unfortunate reply. She put the president's clothes, which she had brought in from the spacious wardrobe down the hall, on the floor as he dashed, as well as his aged form would allow, to the bathroom. The president sighed desperately as he gazed at his brand new face in the bathroom mirror. His eyes had failed and been replaced many times before, and for reasons unconfirmed they'd always been blue. The quality and shade of blue had varied from pair to pair, but blue they had been and this brown, discoloured combo wasn't at all as nice. Nor had the man in the mirror shaved for a while. The reflection appeared to the Yellow Orang-Utan president as slightly monstrous. Gertrude moved his clothes towards the bathroom door while the nude president pressed buttons on his shower, fans whirred and lasers buzzed and he became clean and shaven. He walked out of the bathroom and Gertrude helped dress him. They would proceed to the board room where a breakfast of reptile eggs on toast would be ready to eat. While watching the president wake up Gertrude had decided that she would introduce Wellington to her friends. She did up the president's top button. The time was nine forty-two.

At ten fifty that morning the president was lying on his bed reading another report from the pile Gertrude had collected together from print outs created in a printer room away from any computer. The pile was telling him a wonderful story, voices of characters from a choice variety of departments from inside the building and out. Some had new jargon but contained helpful glossaries, the president read them with a frown. He read them all with a frown, the story was told wonderfully but it was about dark times for Yellow Orang–Utan, they were tales of negative market reactions to Zabdiel Seinfeld, of low opinion polls, of predictions for the company's future. He was alone in the room without Gertrude's company. He was getting very pensive and thoughtful, but continued to read until he started to feel like it was time to lunch. That feeling brought him salivation and he was very near the bottom of the pile after all, the time was six past noon.

At thirty-nine minutes past twelve Gertrude joined the president of Yellow Orang-Utan industries in the boardroom. He was already stuck into his chicken. Gertrude had a pastry on a plate meant for her and she couldn't make out if it was supposed to be hot or cold. She removed a small portion of the pastry with some nearby cutlery. The president paused with his mouth full to watch her test the temperature. He had on the table by his plate a report, the final of the pile from his bed. He browsed it while smearing it with greasy finger marks and chewing mouthfuls of the chicken on his plate, occasionally he'd eat a mushroom that sat around the edges of the dead bird.

"Things are not bearing well for Yellow Orang-Utan, Gertrude. They haven't looked this bad in years, not ever" the president announced after politely swallowing. Gertrude looked up at him, mild interest on her face. He'd watched relevant news sites between reports to get little bits of to-the-minute information about his company and its new president.

The atmosphere of the boardroom was a bit dismal, the pair ate in mostly silence. Gertrude had not reacted much to the president's announcement, she didn't consider it her business. She had been to visit Pepito on one of the lower floors and report her decision to him. She had him leave his workstation and his younger co-workers to speak to her, they made foolish intimations about him and the beauty as he followed her out the door.

"So," the little old man at one end of the boardroom table began, when his plate was all but bones and half a mushroom. "There're big decisions to be made, I have to make them," he continued with a concise exhalation. Gertrude listened carefully, anticipating instructions.

"Please call the cleaner up to take care of the dishes, and do not disturb me until two O' clock, okay?" he pushed his chair out from the table but did not stand.

"Yes sir." Gertrude was still finishing her lunch and remained seated. She watched him, with her mouth full, stand and then exit the room, disappearing into the hall. He walked well, with unusually good posture, Gertrude thought to herself. Although at twelve seconds and thirty-four minutes past twelve she couldn't see him beyond the fine dark wood door of the boardroom to double check.

Gertrude was sitting near a vending machine on one of the orthopaedic chairs ubiquitous throughout the company building at two past two that afternoon. She was just about to notice the time and return to the president's room. Before that however, she was reading a message from Prudence and checking other messages she'd made to herself on her clip-board. She wanted to assure her friends that she was alright despite last time they caught up, she had left their club with the disgusting bed-robed man without polite farewells. Then Gertrude noticed the time and went on to the president's room.

While she did that the president was striding towards his desk. One of the important e-mails he'd received today was from the IT laboratory of Yellow Orang-Utan Industries. It was some new software. The software was meant for the internal network of Yellow Orang-Utan, and would be controlled only by the most important leaders of the corporation, mostly him, the original president who the public were told had passed away. Senior members of the various departments of the building got to access this particular software, but only to make requests, requests concerning the actions of Zabdiel Seinfeld, the president of Yellow Orang-Utan Industries. Because it was with this software that a former president of Yellow Orang-Utan would control a new one, and other software was to come.

It was this software the president was operating when Gertrude arrived back in his room.

"I'm going to terminate some contracts," was the way he put it to Gertrude who sat on the other side of his room. Gertrude looked at a man behind his desk quietly assuring herself that he'd always need her assistance. The president pushed some buttons and made things happen.

"I think," began the president, trying to justify himself to the witnesses. "That after the Diana effect, after Piano died, we got stuck thinking things would always be that good. But that was unprecedented success for Yellow Orang-Utan, we'd never had it that good and we can't expect it to be again, for a while. We will eventually do better, of course, the revolution of Yellow Orang-Utan ensures that. But I fear that we've grown too comfortable in our success and got sluggish. We've got to tighten up. I'm going to make sure every department knows that. The glory days, the success of the Piano years will be heralded as golden in our memories, but I was once president too, I started the company what's more. And I'm afraid Zabdiel Seinfeld is going to have to show people that. Piano Smedley is dead and he, like our recent success, is not forever lasting. I'm afraid Seinfeld's going to be a little tougher. I was tough once too, neither of us will ever be as lovable as Smedley if we tried. So I'm going to terminate some contracts."

The president pressed more buttons to make more things happen. It was having repercussions. People in other parts of the building were beginning to talk to the president, Zabdiel Seinfeld. It was comparatively quiet in the room of the Yellow Orang-Utan president with a biological form, you could hear the president breathing and Gertrude move across the floor to a comfy cushion near the Wall-span TV. A little while later the man at the desk facing the on-screen software interface that controlled the multifaceted Zabdiel Seinfeld corporate president paused before clicking on something.

"It's just...I think I personally, having to deal with all this nonsense when he died, I mean. It's not what Yellow Orang-Utan is about, it's all just extra, you know? I created Yellow Orang-Utan, it was my idea and then we made Piano and then the idea ballooned and got bigger and everybody loved it and we became the biggest company in the world and we made billions and trillions all the time. But we've gathered up all this other stuff over time, to be like our competitors, all the extra stuff that comes along with being a giant corporation. And dealing with that stuff, all that other stuff, if you strip it all away we've still got Yellow Orang-Utan, that's what makes us special, it's what changed everything forever, it's beautiful. But it's that other stuff that's had us lose sight of what Yellow Orang-Utan really, actually is, you know?" blubbered the president, still justifying his button pushing to the gorgeous woman watching him in his room.

"We've let go of the core that was holding us together and making us great," he added. Gertrude blankly eyed the man behind the desk. The time was two fifteen.

At two nineteen, after one of the lead market-hackers had got off the phone with Zabdiel Seinfeld, another phone rang in the office of Naamah Nelise, a vice president of Yellow Orang-Utan Industries and she answered the ring.

"Hello, Naamah Nelise speaking," she said politely into the phone mouthpiece. It was Zabdiel Seinfeld. He gave a speech that was very similar in sentiment to that given to Gertrude during the previous minutes, although with more conviction and sounding better rehearsed. He informed Naamah of his intentions for Yellow Oran-Utan and what he had planned. That he'd already been calling the heads of departments and letting them know that they weren't to expect with smug security another windfall like the Diana effect too soon. That it was time to put noses to grindstones and shape up. He wanted more frequent activity reports to create more transparency and cohesion between the departments and senior management. Then Zabdiel Seinfeld told Naamah about his intentions to terminate contracts of Yellow Orang-Utan employees. Naamah heard very clearly their names and positions.

"Are you sure?" she asked the president hesitantly.

"I certainly feel something to that effect must be done," answered Seinfeld.

"To be quite frank, Zabdiel, I think you're making a big mistake." Zabdiel Seinfeld made strong counter arguments for every point Naamah had over the next intense few minutes, he was designed to. Naamah gave up the fight and backed down. The phone call ended with greetings that carried the courtesy that ensured positive business relations. Fingernails of the vice president were already in her mouth when her receiver was returned to its proper resting place. She stood up out of her chair and backed against the wall. She felt exasperated, then the phone rang again.

"Naamah? It's Letitia," Naamah heard when she picked up the phone. She knew there'd be nothing left to do but warn them now, similar calls would be received any second now in nearby offices. A tiny clock on her computer screen indicated the time was two-twenty three.

At two-twenty four the phone rang in Jacobo's office, his feet were resting on his horoscope coffee table, on the sign for Libra. He put down the report he was perusing and went to the phone console, he saw the light flash that indicated the call was presidential.

"Hello, Zabdiel?" Jacobo enquired through the phone. Today he was wearing a visibly uncomfortable, small suit.

"Hello Jacobo," answered Zabdiel. Jacobo was to be made even more uncomfortable very quickly.

"What do you want to do today?" Jacobo returned.

"This is really uncomfortable for me to do, Jacobo. I'm afraid I'm terminating your contract with Yellow Orang-Utan." Zabdiel allowed a pause for the shocking news to sink into Jacobo.

"Effective at the end of the month, not immediately. I still need your quality input in the running of Yellow Orang-Utan during this beginning of my term as president." Zabdiel was calm and comforting in his slow, deliberate speech.

"Has it to do with my performance?" Jacobo nervously enquired to the fake president Jacobo worked to install.

"No, this is a reflection of my intentions for Yellow Orang-Utan, my regime," answered Zabdiel, with a sigh.

"Thank you for the notice, Mr. Seinfeld," finished Jacobo.

"You're going to be OK," assured the voice from Jacobo's phone. "OK? Goodbye."

"Bye," Jacobo pressed a button that ended his conversation. The polite conversation was over now and the phone dangled from Jacobo's limp limb. He'd sit down again soon, but he wouldn't put his feet up. He needed to sit down to grasp the news with the right cocktail of emotions, but at two thirty-five, that was still forthcoming.

At two thirty-two Oakley was on an important phone call and had Palmira take his incoming calls. This was when Zabdiel Seinfeld called.

"Hello, Oakley Oades' office, Palmira speaking," announced Palmira. He agreed to hold while waiting for Oakley to be available to talk. Oakley took down the details with his silver pen about the call's business before ending his important phone call. He received information from Palmira that Zabdiel was holding on one of his phone lines and he took the call, greeting Zabdiel cordially. Today he wore his pink shirt.

"I can be straightforward with you Oakley, I'm looking to make some dramatic changes to Yellow Orang-Utan. I think we've been resting on our laurels too much and have grown stale. I want a shake up. I want to reinvigorate Yellow Orang-Utan and change the way people look at us. It's only early days now, but I'm confident we can make some positive new directions…" was something Zabdiel had to say.

"And?" probed Oakley, who was familiar with this pattern of speech, he often used it himself.

"I'm beginning by creating an all new board of executive directors," answered Seinfeld, not a quiver in his voice. Oakley breathed through gritted teeth, Zabdiel's news was just as Naamah had said on his previous call.

"I'm terminating your contract with Yellow Orang-Utan Industries," reported the president of Yellow Orang-Utan Industries.

"So what do I have coming to me?" asked Oakley, assessing his situation.

"You have until the end of the month, then of course a board member does not go away without a bountiful redundancy package," came

Seinfeld's calculatedly polite reply.

"I guess I could thank you for being so forthright," said Oakley, although this seemed almost a joke to both interacting through the phone line, except one merely gave the impression without understanding the humour.

"Would I be able to apply for a position on the new board?" Oakley continued.

"You, Oakley, you would certainly be welcome back, or at least, strongly considered when we assemble the new board," was the token automated response, customised for Oakley, the Yellow Orang-Utan Industries executive board member. He let the phone conversation come to its natural, patterned conclusion before following it up with another call.

He smiled, it was answered by a former employer and an old friend. He explained his call and relayed the news of his finite time at Yellow Orang-Utan Industries. He intimated his future availability to his former employer, who became audibly excited. They laughed and exchanged personal stories for a few minutes before Oakley ended the call, explaining he still was busy in his current position. At the other end of the phone line, a tired guy breathed a sigh of relief at the thought of having Oakley back in his life, there weren't many like Oakley.

Oakley glanced over at the picture of his family, he'd be letting them know of his latest unfortunate development that evening, he'd be very deliberate. His brow looked pensive, unusual for Oakley, and his shiny pine furniture seemed to have lost its sheen momentarily. The sudden upset had yet to affect this entire floor of the Yellow Orang-Utan building's occupants at two forty-four and forty-three seconds.

Queenie answered a phone call for Kal-El at two thirty-nine.

"Hello this is Kal-El Ka's office, Queenie speaking," she announced.

"Hello Queenie, this is Zabdiel Seinfeld" came a voice through the phone.

"Oh, Mr. Seinfeld, sir! I'm afraid Kal-El's not in at the moment," she responded.

"Really, where is he?"

"You could probably reach him on his mobile," Queenie said quickly.

"Oh, alright, I'll try that, thank you Queenie," said Zabdiel Seinfeld. Queenie hung up the phone quickly, relieved the phone conversation was over. She resumed her e-mail monitoring at two forty and fifty seconds.

At two forty and thirty-five seconds Kal-El's phone buzzed in his pocket. He was in a meeting with two cheery faced other gentlemen. Today the Yellow Orang-Utan Industries board member wore gel in his hair and a conservatively plain but still customarily baggy suit. The pair had travelled a long way to meet with a representative from Yellow Orang-Utan Industries.

Kal-El had helped negotiate this meeting and the contract they were eager to sign, whereby Yellow Orang-Utan Industries would own the product of their life's largest endeavour. He politely signalled to the other two gentlemen assembled that he'd received a call and answered the buzzing phone.

"Hello? Kal-El speaking," answered Kal-El into his communicating device.

"Uh-huh, hello sir," he continued. He listened to the president of Yellow Orang-Utan Industries speaking for a moment.

"Can I call you back? I'm about to sign a contract with Ebert Ea and Fabian Faaborg from Dorrington Boa." Kal-El requested. The two gentlemen heard the muffled speaker vibrate against Kal-El's ear.

"Dorrington Boa," Kal-El repeated, with more careful annunciation.

"I'm at the *Confucius Hotel*," Kal-El told Zabdiel Seinfeld, who then agreed to Kal-El's request. The phone call over, Kal-El smiled at the two businessmen, who were already smiling back. Kal-El and the others used brand new pens to sign the contract. They clinked another group of liquid filled glasses to celebrate the deal at three fifty-seven in the afternoon.

At two forty-two and ten seconds one of the two correctly working telephones rang in Rahel's office. She glanced at the phone, she was already operating the second phone.

"That could be him now," she exclaimed.

"What?" asked Naamah, through the connected phone line.

"My phone's ringing, my other phone is ringing right now, I have to go," Rahel announced.

"Oh, Rahel I'm so sorry about this," Naamah finished. Rahel only half heard her as she put one receiver down while lifting the other.

"Good afternoon, Rahel, this is the president," announced Zabdiel Seinfeld.

"Oh, hello sir, how are you, Mr. Seinfeld?" Rahel politely replied.

"I'm alright," Zabdiel said carefully, "but I'm afraid I have some unpleasant news."

"Oh, really?" said Rahel, disappointed to have her new suspicions so quickly confirmed.

"I'm replacing the board of directors at Yellow Orang-Utan, which includes you and all the others. It's a difficult thing to do, it's a controversial thing to do, but I want to make my direction clear concerning Yellow Orang-Utan's future," explained Seinfeld.

"I understand," Rahel slowly exhaled and looked at her pin-board.

"There'll be a generous redundancy package, naturally," assured the fake president of Yellow Orang-Utan Industries.

"Well I'm glad to hear that," Rahel replied, trying to raise her spirits and change her attitude to the news.

"And it's not until the end of the month," added Zabdiel, reading the tone in Rahel in an unavoidably artificial way.

"OK, that would make the transition easier," piped in Rahel, glad the president could assist in her own train of thought. She wore a light grey skirt and pale yellow shirt today.

"It's a shame we haven't really got the chance to work with you for any extended period of time," Rahel said, almost teasing herself as well as the president of Yellow Orang-Utan Industries, Zabdiel Seinfeld. "We're missing out on the chance to work together on some new endeavours."

"Hmm, that's certainly a loss worth thinking of, but I don't think it will affect my decision at this time," Seinfeld returned, a touch of humour to his voice as well.

"But I'm afraid I do have to go now Rahel, I am the busy new president after all, sorry this phone call couldn't be more pleasant," finished the president, pleasantly.

"Alright, goodbye Mr. Seinfeld. I hope to hear from you again before the end of the month," farewelled Rahel.

"I hope so too, Rahel, goodbye" farewelled Zabdiel Seinfeld. Rahel put the phone receiver down on its corresponding phone, she picked up the other, Namaah had heard the whole conversation. They kept talking, Rahel sighed and looked at her pin-board of favourite cartoons, they probably wouldn't cheer her up today. Namaah assured her she was taking the news rather well, and that she could take advantage of that. They ended the conversation, Namaah wanted to keep calling the other board members and Rahel wanted to wander their floor of the building, find them and discuss in person what was happening. With all her receivers back on their respective phones, including the one that didn't work anymore Rahel turned back to the report she was reading before all the phone calls. She thought it best to finish reading it before venturing outside her air-conditioned office, that she still had until the end of the month, because this too was her responsibility until then. The time was two fifty-three.

At two forty-seven Sabra pressed a button on her ringing phone and answered the call.

"Hello," she cooed into the speakerphone.

"Hello Sabra," issued from the speaker in reply, "Zabdiel Seinfeld here." Sabra moved a strand of her hair behind her ear before she answered, nervously.

"What do you want to do today, sir?" she asked, returning to her office couch where she perched carefully above documents spread out over its upholstery.

"Unfortunately I have some bad news for you, Sabra," said Sabra's phone.

"Oh? What could that be?" asked Sabra, deciding not to pay attention.

"I'm terminating your contract with Yellow Orang-Utan Industries," Zabdiel announced officially. Sabra paused. The flowers she'd been sent recently blurred past her eyes as she turned towards the phone.

"What?" She asked, taken aback.

"I'm terminating your contract with Yellow Orang-Utan Industries," the president said again.

"I'm sorry?" asked Sabra again, trying to grasp the concept. The voice emanating from the phone paused, not risking repeating itself again.

"I'm sorry, you're trying to terminate my contract?"

"Yes," answered Zabdiel Seinfeld, which seemed kind of blunt to Sabra.

"No," said Sabra.

"It's unfortunate for you I know, but I'm replacing the entire board of directors at Yellow Orang-Utan Industries," offered Zabdiel.

"You can't do that,"' exclaimed Sabra.

"It is my decision and my prerogative," answered Zabdiel Seinfeld before continuing, "there'll be a generous redundancy package, and this is not effective until the end of the month. I'm sorry Sabra."

"Oh, don't apologise Seinfeld," Sabra snapped back angrily. "It wasn't so long ago that this board of directors were overseeing your existence, now you, or more correctly someone like you is giving us the flick and hiding behind you like a rotten coward."

"Sabra, I think you know very well that I'm the legitimate president of Yellow Orang-Utan Industries and can and will make decisions affecting you and the entire company."

"I invented your name, Zabdiel Seinfeld! You were going to be Vail Shamrock!" Sabra cried in a huff, the blood between her face and skull made her glow. The phone representing the voice of Zabdiel Seinfeld, formerly Vail Shamrock, didn't respond.

"What have we done to deserve this?" She demanded with a hint of desolation.

"This has nothing to do with your performance, nor anyone else on the board, this is my decision, mine alone. It has more to do with my new vision for Yellow Orang-Utan, it shouldn't be surprising, I am a new president," blabbed Sabra's phone. Sabra swore in response, she wanted to plead with the powerful leader, but it was kind of silly, due to its power as much as the false impersonation. Instead, she sat with her arms folded, scowling.

"Sabra?" called Zabdiel Seinfeld through her phone, there had been a brief uncomfortable silence.

"Sabra, I still require your valuable services until the end of the month. I think I've made myself clear. Are we on the same level, huh? Is my reason for calling understood?" asked Seinfeld. Sabra breathed audibly.

"Sabra?" volunteered the president.

"Fine, go," called Sabra. Her speakerphone began beeping until Sabra reached up and pressed a button to change its beeping status. The papers she'd been perusing on her couch had been crumpled after being distracted by the phone call. She wandered into her secretary's office to let him know what had happened, and that he'd lose his job too. She'd never argued like that with Piano Smedley. Nobody had. And that began to worry her as she disappeared once more into her office. Her cat shaped clock indicated it was five to three.

The time was six minutes to three in the afternoon, at this time a phone rang in Taggart's office. Taggart answered the call.

"Hello, Taggart speaking," Taggart said into his telephone receiver.

"Hello Taggart, this is Zabdiel Seinfeld," said a synthesised voice to Taggart. Taggart stroked his moustache and looked around his office for his cup of coffee.

"What do you want to do today, sir?" he asked sarcastically.

"I want to give you some news, Taggart," replied Zabdiel Seinfeld. Taggart had an inkling it would be bad news and said so.

"I'd like to say you're wrong, Taggart, but I'm afraid you're too perceptive," admitted Seinfeld.

"Unfortunately I've decided to replace Yellow Orang-Utan Industries board of executive directors and I'm terminating your contract at the end of the month," the president's news didn't come clearly to Taggart because he had dashed to the other side of his office to fetch his cup of coffee. He'd also heard from Letitia Bjorksdotter, vice president of Yellow Orang-Utan Industies several minutes before this call and understood clearly what the direction of the conversation was and didn't particularly care for it.

"Sorry, I didn't catch that?" He said when he got back to the receiver. Zabdiel repeated his news to the man with hot coffee on his tongue. The man let the coffee stay in his mouth for a moment longer than he was accustomed. Eventually he swallowed.

"Uh, huh," was his slow verbal reaction.

"Uh, there'll be a bountiful redundancy package," added Zabdiel, unsure how to read Taggart's reaction. Taggart had already added losing his job to the beleaguered list of reasons his life was at its worst that year.

"You haven't been here long enough to really know this is the right decision. You don't know how much the board is behind making Yellow Orang-Utan as strong as it is," argued Taggart. There was a slight pause to Zabdiel Seinfeld's response. Taggart inhaled his coffee steam through his nose.

"Uh, huh," retorted the bored sounding Taggart. Taggart ended the conversation with Zabdiel Seinfeld deftly after that.

He moaned eloquently and sat in his chair. He looked around his office and realised he'd have to shift all his furniture out at the end of the month. His bookshelves would all have to be unpacked. He pulled a hand over his face, this he didn't need. He managed to laugh in between muttering swear words. Then he finished his coffee. The time by then was five minutes past three.

At twenty-eight minutes past three, there was a loud crash in the Yellow Orang-Utan Industries building. Before the loud crash, board members and their secretaries had gathered in Calandré and Taggart's offices to discuss the news of their terminated contracts. Letitia had come down there and Sabra and her similarly sacked secretary, Quenby, ventured over there too. Namaah, having got the impression that the word had spread everywhere it needed to, made another call to Oakley, who was still working but had passed on the news to Palmira, who quickly told Queenie. Rahel told her secretary Baudric, who decided he'd go find something to eat. Karel went over to Queenie's office to enquire about some business and he learned of the day's strange and sudden developments there. He went back to his office and poked his head in Jacobo's door, after politely knocking, and saw his boss sitting in silence. He knew enough about the man in the tight fitting suit to guess he had heard the same news he'd just got from Queenie and Palmira, so he returned to his work. Rahel found Palmira and Queenie together and they all went to Calandré's office, then some assembled there meandered into Taggart's when he poked his head through the door into Calandré's. Taggart was topping up his coffee pot when everyone on that floor heard a loud crash.

It was significant enough a sound for Oakley to stop what he was doing and wander out through Palmira's office into the hall to find its source. When he saw Karel's face as Karel dashed out of his office and ran toward Palmira, who stood in the doorway of Calandré's office, Oakley quickly made a call to security.

"Jacobo's just smashed open his window, he's out on the ledge!" Karel reported in short breaths. People in Calandre's office gasped. Rahel dashed up to Jacobo's office. Karel moved deeper into the assembly to tell those in Taggart's office too. People followed Karel as he made his way back to his end of the building. Oakley heard what was happening and made another call to security. He wanted to be confident his excellent negotiating skills would be sufficient for the situation, but he didn't want to take that chance and requested a specific professional.

Rahel was in Jacobo's office. The wind from that height whipped in and Jacobo's loose papers were pinned against the high reaches of his office walls, as were his decorative foil pillows. Rahel was on the ledge outside Jacobo's office. She had climbed over a few bits of broken glass to get there, although most of it had travelled to the ground far below, settling next to a fragmented coffee table.

"Jacobo?" She called.

"The breeze is nice," Jacobo barked. The wind was really strong, Rahel's hair was stinging her eyes as strands sailed into them. Jacobo didn't have any hair.

"Jacobo, please come inside," Rahel had to say.

"My life is over," Jacobo replied, after an appropriately dramatic pause.

"It is far from that," insisted Rahel.

"No...I loved this company," said Jacobo, and he meant it.

"You've got more than the company. People love you, Jacobo. You've got family and friends who really, really want you to come back inside." Rahel bit her lip, scared she'd been picking the wrong words.

"No, no it's a joke. I...I've been cheating on my wife, Rahel. It's been going on for close to a year, and it's not the first time." Jacobo announced emotionally. Rahel's mouth dropped open.

"I've ruined it for me and Bek time and time again. And it's a joke, none of them came even close to being as good as her, but I keep doing it, and this one's been going on for nearly a year...and she's a joke." Jacobo finished then Rahel felt her guts churn out on the ledge, this was startling news to her, she hadn't a thing left to say. Because she'd forgotten exactly how long she'd wanted desperately to be his, and she hated that this was a moment where she was reflecting on that, and the time was three thirty-five.

At six forty-four and ten seconds, the president sat alone in his room watching Telly-net. He was watching the news. The president was seated reasonably comfortably on his bed, he had a glass of milk nearby to drink and make him feel good. He would have a mouthful, lick his upper lip clean of remaining liquid, then resume frowning. That Zabdiel Seinfeld had today fired his company's board of directors had been announced following the close of the business day. A media release had been issued from the offices of the board earlier that day. Now images, sound bytes and obligatory references back to Piano Smedley were being edited together in an informative and entertaining format for Telly-net users. Someone at *Fishpaste* would be resting their drink on it. Expert opinion was presented by well-dressed and educated professionals spouting polite sentences that simplified the situation from its wider context. He kept watching, and frowning, for hours and hours, until seventeen minutes past eleven that night.

12.

Usually you're forced to pick the best of several goods, or the least bad of several evils.

At ten to two in the afternoon the president of Yellow Orang-Utan Industries watched his beautiful assistant Gertrude exit his room, at his request. He'd been having his usual post-lunch discussion with Gertrude about his business and his intentions for the afternoon. But now the discussed afternoon was upon him and he should get down to his post-preamble business. He sat at a desk he considered his own and examined files about potential new members for Zabdiel Seinfeld's new board of directors. They had come to him filtered through the offices of Namaah Nelise and Letitia Bjorksdotter, the vice presidents of Yellow Orang-Utan Industries, as well as senior officials from various departments of the company. Soon a select bunch mentioned and recommended by these files would present themselves to a screen bearing the image of Zabdiel Seinfeld and they would appear to be talking to him, as he would them. Such a senior position is a highly valued prize to many but it had only been possessed by very few.

The files were very interesting, but during a brief point of disinterest for the president, he allowed himself to lean back, stretch, and his mind to wander. It wandered to Zabdiel Seinfeld's television appearances since firing the previous board of directors. Yellow Orang-Utan's PR department had carefully scripted each appearance. Zabdiel handled the famous Telly-net journalists' questions easily. But this didn't stop negative speculation from every relevant media personality, nor the president frowning long into the night while he watched the news media. He'd instructed the PR department to develop another Telly-net appearance that morning. He'd see it on his big screen in a day or so. He lamented that his train of thought had stayed so dutifully on his affairs without any more whimsical tangents, but conceded it was probably in his interests. He resumed examining the files of prospective new members of Yellow Orang-Utan Industries board of directors. The time was two O' clock and forty-six minutes.

At twenty past six Gertrude met Wellington by his office in the market hacking department of the Yellow Orang-Utan Industries building. She'd had to ride elevators past many different levels of the big building and then follow signs carefully to find his office. It was not somewhere she frequented.

"Hallo Gertrude," greeted Wellington with a friendly smile.

"Hi," replied Gertrude, sounding a little tired. She was but she had already agreed to take Wellington out tonight.

"Are you ready to go?" she asked. Beyond his greeting Wellington appeared to be preoccupied by the goings on around his offices' computer screen.

"Yes, I just need to finish one quick thing," he said. He clicked a few buttons before rising. His clothes were very smooth with barely a wrinkle on them, Gertrude wore more wrinkles than he amongst a faux wooly skirt and jacket and a very small top. Her hair was adorned with glittery decorations. The pair exited the office and made their way to the ground floor of the building.

"Is this the first time you've left the building?" asked Gertrude when they stepped outside into the darkening sky.

"Yes," answered Wellington, matter-of-factly. He looked at Gertrude with a blank smile.

"You say that like I'm an agoraphobic," Wellington suggested humorously. They continued down the street.

"Will the change in atmosphere affect your body at all?" asked Gertrude.

"I shouldn't think so," he said. They used the inter city transport services to take them to a popular dining district. The interiors of the restaurants shone on Gertrude and Wellington as they walked along the streets and Gertrude decided where they would eat. She calculated the pleasure each venue could provide as she glanced at their advertising. She settled on *Bastion*, an upmarket though modest venue that sold dishes that sat inconspicuously and comfortably within the overwhelming assortment of the world's foods. They had to wait for a while to be seated.

"You can eat, can't you?" Gertrude enquired.

"I can certainly give that impression," Wellington said, quietly, intimating to Gertrude it might not be best to question his robotic status in a busy restaurant. When they were seated and handed menus Wellington asked about Gertrude. Gertrude told him that she'd returned to working with the president after the time off he'd known about.

"Well, I haven't been here before, what do you recommend?" asked Wellington.

"I've only been here a few times myself, depends what you feel like," Gertrude replied. On one dish she remarked:

"I quite like that but it's usually clone meat."

"What is?" forwarded Wellington.

"The macaw," Gertrude replied. There was a comfortable menu reading silence.

"Their vendors have random functions, I think I'll just go for that," Wellington announced.

"I feel like something with tomatoes, I think I'll have the pasta. I might have had some of that last time and it was good. Very chunky." Gertrude put her menu down. Wellington pressed a few buttons on the control pad for the vendors on his table. Bastion was filled with the sound of diners talking, waiting, eating and music playing in the kitchen. Gertrude motioned a waiter over to order her meal, the waiter pressed buttons for her. Wellington looked at the food emerging from the vendors near the kitchen, anticipating the appearance of his dish.

"Do you watch much Telly-net?" asked Wellington, sounding hopeful. This was one topic he could possibly discuss without having to lie about his experiences, but he could premeditate Gertrude's answer based on memories he still had stored.

"No, I tend to go out a lot," was Gertrude's predictable response.

"A lot of restaurant dining?" Wellington suggested.

"No, I cook at home. Sometimes I eat out with friends, or occasionally my boss has me out to the Swinging Hanky. But usually I eat at home."

Gertrude looked at Wellington probing her for information, she recognised that was what he was up to. But she admitted to herself this would be the practice of anyone on an outing with her for the first time, their behaviour matched multiple other couples across the restaurant floor. She accepted this and locked herself on to his gaze and continued to tell her story. Wellington would even grin on the verge of laughter at anecdotes Gertrude had always thought funny, even if they'd had a 'you had to be there' status in other circumstances. This went very well then a waiter brought a dish for Wellington to the table. It was a soup. Wellington continued to survey Gertrude's life and opinions in between mouthfuls. He offered some soup to Gertrude. She tried it. It had been enticing while she was waiting and a bit spicy after the first mouthful went down, yummy.

"It's very good," she said.

"Mmm," agreed Wellington half-heartedly, not being able to taste anything. Not long after that Gertrude's pasta arrived at the table. It was chunky, as she had guessed it would be. They talked about their respective dishes between mouthfuls. Wellington's soup was joined by a bread and meat dish, Gertrude ordered a dessert pre-empting the arrival of Wellington's third course. Gertrude remained in the full attention of Wellington, and he her, as they continued to chat through dinner.

"I'm having fun, Wellington, and the food here is good." She had to eventually concede. Her mistrust was disappearing as the feast went on, her analytical approach to him was losing its grip.

"I'm having a good time, too" echoed Wellington. Wellington's investigation of Gertrude had investigative returns from Gertrude.

"Wait," said Gertrude, interrupting one of Wellington's answers. Wellington had been telling a lie.

"That can't have happened," Gertrude's analytical, mistrustful side crept back up again.

"Well no, but pretend it did, OK?" Wellington said, hushing the conversation. Wellington had a fake history of experiences programmed into him, a lot of them he shared with his inventor, Pepito. He used them to tell stories to Gertrude about his past, Wellington explained, humorously. Gertrude accepted the explanation. She exhaled loudly.

"Then what happened after you got back to the hotel?" Gertrude asked to prompt Wellington's story. They continued in a familiarly pleasant vein for the rest of the evening, through dessert, as they paid before leaving the restaurant, then onward out into the street. They rode back to the Yellow Orang-Utan Industries building, talking audibly for other passengers to hear, Gertrude more so than Wellington. They walked back to Wellington's quarters, their very tall work building, from the station.

"Thank you very much for escorting me out tonight, Gertrude," Wellington said gleefully.

"Oh, no worries, Wellington, we can do it again any time," Gertrude replied. Wellington and she took a hold of the other's corresponding hands and shook them while they gazed happily into each other's eyes. Wellington let go of Gertrude's hand.

"Goodbye," he said before venturing back inside the building he was most familiar with.

"Bye," called Gertrude, waving. She walked to another station and rode back to her home. She smiled to herself thinking of different prospective social scenarios she could introduce to the entertaining robot as she got off the transport and walked to her door. Then she'd arrived, the time was eight minutes to ten.

At nine O' clock in the evening and thirty-two minutes the president of Yellow Orang-Utan Industries lay in his bed and watched Telly-net. He was settled into the frowning expression he'd developed from watching Telly-net over the recent past. He'd eaten healthy food during the day, he'd even had an expertly delivered massage that morning and the examination of potential new board members via files prepared in an easy to read fashion was hardly a stressful day's work. These did nothing to prevent the frown.

He adjusted his position in his bed and sighed. News of the day, in the president of Yellow Orang-Utan Industries' world was relatively historic. The stock market value of shares owned by investors in his company had gone down today. This was the first time they had decreased in value for many years. It wasn't a worry compared with other stock market fluctuations, Yellow Orang-Utan Industries was still the biggest company in the world and their stock still very valuable. But the mystery of why it had gone down would concern the new president Zabdiel Seinfeld, who was replacing the company's board of directors. Media professionals on the Telly-net news sites long into the night repeatedly bandied about this information. The president sat through as much as he could bear before becoming too tired. The carafe of water he could serve himself with by his bed didn't keep him up any longer than naturally allowed by his body. He switched off the enormous Wall-span TV at twelve minutes past ten.

13.

How could they forsake their living, and their own family and friends, without even giving notice, to follow this strange stranger and his motley crue?

Memos were received and read by employees of Yellow Orang-Utan Industries at nine O' three in the morning. They were from Zabdiel Seinfeld. He was contacting the relevant departments whose performance had suffered during the transfer of the board of directors. The message was an attempt to persuade the people working at each department to apply themselves better than they had lately, presuming the suffering performances were a result of their supposed directors shirking off their duties as they prepared to exit their positions. As the message was passed on to them from their bosses and other managers, some of the harder working employees secretly thought this wasn't necessarily the case. However, Zabdiel remained the persuasive president he was supposed to be, and these workers were ultimately inclined to agree to his request. The physical president was immediately oblivious to the memo received by his underlings. He was previously aware when he arranged for Zabdiel to make the memo the evening before. He was awake then, just now he was sound asleep in his bed – around ten past nine in the morning.

At approximately nine twenty-nine and forty-four seconds Gertrude entered the president's bedroom.

"Good morning sir, what do you want to do today?" she piped, slightly arousing the president.

"Good morning Gertrude, please get me some coffee," was his polite return, that he half groaned as he struggled to get up. Gertrude fetched the coffee and the president began to drink it. As he drank he remembered the memo he'd organised to be sent this morning from Zabdiel Seinfeld. The memo was timed to coincide with the arrival of the new board of executive directors. They were officially acting as the new board today. The old board's offices were now clear and some of the new board had been busying themselves in there the week before. Today they would make formal introductions to the company's departments, many of which they now had a measure of control over. They would be reviewing the status and directions of their predecessors' labours and considering what could be improved upon and enhanced. They'd also consider ways to personalise their offices and whom they may hire to help them. Most of them were enthusiastic to be working for Yellow Orang-Utan Industries, the biggest company in the world and couldn't possibly secure a better job than this for the rest of their career. This echoed the sentiment of some of the old board. The president took another sip of his coffee.

He asked Gertrude about any possible appointments and engagements he had to attend to today. She kept him up to date and informed while he continued sipping coffee and thinking about the new board. A consolidated media release about the arrival of the new board was in pre-production the week before and would be ready for the media's consumption within the next forty-eight hours. Not long after that it would be assumed there would be a television appearance with Zabdiel and the board together. That was in pre-emptive pre-production, the public relations people would be scripting it today.

"And then you can look at the drafts for that this afternoon as well as completing the background reports on the new board." Gertrude had finished and had advanced some of the beliefs the president had of his company that day. He hadn't even finished coffee yet. He'd assume it was to be a good day were it not for the bad news he'd surveyed every night lately. But then again, Yellow Orang-Utan would be striking the media with their own news this week so things could be panning out for the better. The time was nine forty.

It was eight forty-nine when the president of Yellow Orang-Utan Industries got back to his room after dining out at *The Swinging Hanky*. He had been feeling confident for most of the day and wanted to face the news of the new board on the Telly-net without a frown. He had caught up with some of his mogul peers there. Their supportive remarks were still fresh in his mind as he pressed the buttons on his remote control to fill his mind with less sociable sound bytes. He watched stories of ghastly accidents in far away lands while he dressed slowly into nudity, then into pyjamas Gertrude had laid on his bed for him before she left. He wasn't frowning yet, but his smile had dropped slightly being distracted by his dressing task and the images. He climbed into his endlessly comfortable bed and his smile returned as the furniture embraced him. The president's attention returned to the Wall-span TV and he flicked amongst the news sites to find news of his giant corporation's new board of directors.

He found a little but not a lot, it wasn't the biggest news of the day, not like when Piano died, when the story was pointlessly monitored for hours. The opinionated media personalities involved with news reporting didn't touch upon the story much except to say they wanted to wait and see them perform before casting judgement. He spent a little more time watching, switching over to other sites and waiting for more Yellow Orang-Utan news but it was not to be. He sat despondently for a while, muted the Wall-span, and thought where to go next with a remote control without leaving his bed. Eventually he settled for another attempt at the Piano Smedley biographical movie.

This time he wasn't under the influence of any industrially manufactured drugs and the movie made more sense. Plus his eyes didn't fail during the screening and he could see the whole story. It was a great story with some moments of inspiration that genuinely connected with the president of Yellow Orang-Utan Industries, as they had with its many other viewers. But during its long running time the president found cause to frown a little bit.

He tried to shoo away his mental despondency, reminding himself he'd been working very diligently and he should be proud of that considering the mess he'd made of himself in his time off. And he had been working hard, the reason he again used to explain now why he still hadn't felt any hopeful stirrings in his crotch since coming back from his break, or during, or before. But the less thought about his little penis the better he had concluded, well before the credits rolled on the Piano Smedley biographical movie. Then the credits rolled on the Piano Smedley biographical movie, the time was three minutes past midnight.

At eight thirteen Gertrude met with Wellington at the bottom of the biggest building in the world.

"Hello! Are you ready?" asked a happy Gertrude.

"Of course I am," answered the robot with mirrored happiness. They strolled down to an inner city transport station that would take them to Gertrude's favourite venue, *Fishpaste*. On the way they made the effort to catch up with what the other had been doing in the brief respite they'd had from each other. But that didn't take long and their discussion shifted to anticipations for the evening. They didn't have to stroll very long either, once they hit the street where all manner of amusing evening entertaining venues could be found.

Very soon they were in *Fishpaste*. Gertrude entered with a vigour and freshness she hadn't associated with her more recent visits. Wellington studied the layout of the club carefully, he took in its physical dimensions as well as the information supplied by the ubiquitous screens of the club.

"Gertrude!" loudly called Prudence, Gertrude's friend. She walked across the floor to the newly arrived pair.

"Hi, how are you," continued Prudence in quieter tones up close. She and Gertrude kissed hello.

"This is Wellington. Wellington, Prudence. Prudence, Wellington." Introduced Gertrude.

"How do you do," said Wellington firmly, taking a hold of Prudence's hand.

"I'm doing very well, thank you, yourself?" greeted Prudence.

"I'm in fine form," Wellington replied.

Biscuit sat with Prudence's friends, across the room. When she saw her good friend Gertrude greeting Prudence with the handsome man she ran over to greet her.

"Gertrude!" cooed Biscuit, giving Gertrude a hug.

"Biscoe," Gertrude returned, mid-hug. Prudence and Wellington were already cordially discussing their mutual friend while Biscuit and Gertrude debriefed each other with their latest business. When the quartet ran out of conversation they adopted the new topic of drinks and headed to the bar. Wellington had the same drink as Gertrude, Prudence had a dairy based alcoholic beverage with bright colouring added and Biscuit had a lemonade trying not to mix alcohol with the chemicals in the pill Sensae had given her back at their table. As the four headed back toward the table,

Gertrude introduced Biscuit to Wellington.

"How do you know Gertrude?" asked Biscuit after the introduction.

"Oh, work," said Wellington.

"Yellow Orang-Utan?" asked Biscuit.

"Yes," he replied.

"I work there too," Biscuit exclaimed, "What department do you work for?"

"I'm in market hacking," came Wellington's calm reply.

"I'm in PR," said the secretary. Their conversation topic remained on the things that the two had in common while they seated themselves amongst Biscuit's friends and for some time after that. Biscuit introduced a flirt or two into their discourse, which Wellington would react to pleasantly. Biscuit looked over at Gertrude, who was chatting with Prudence, checking for Gertrude's reaction to her behaviour towards Wellington. Gertrude had already stolen a glance over at the two and been very approving of Wellington's behaviour, as friendly and inviting as his personality was. Biscuit stopped their small talk to introduce Wellington to Sensae. Sensae introduced Wellington and Gertrude to his new friends that he'd also brought along. He always had new people to introduce. Talk continued amongst those gathered for a good while, in between trips to the bar and toilet.

"So, what's the thing you have with Wellington?" asked Biscuit when the two women were leaving the bar, their new drinks in hand.

"We don't have a thing, he's just a friend from work," Gertrude answered with a touch of pride. She looked at Biscuit's Wellington-locked gaze. She got slightly and quickly worried for her friend.

"Biscoe, I don't think–" Gertrude began.

"What?" Biscuit interjected, calling into Gertrude's ear to avoid the din of the nightclub.

"Take it easy with him, be very careful," advised Gertrude loudly into Biscuit's ear. Biscuit gave Gertrude a look that tried to persuade her such caution wasn't necessary and she knew how to handle herself.

"Biscoe," Gertrude said sternly, returning a concerned look.

"What?" said Biscuit again, maintaining her misguided reassuring look.

"Nothing," answered Gertrude, conceding defeat. They returned to the bunch around the table. Wellington was observing one of the moving images on one of the many screens in Fishpaste. Biscuit resumed her position beside him and asked him what he was watching. He pointed to one of the screens.

"Yellow Orang-Utan is in a spot of trouble," he said. Biscuit followed his index but couldn't see anything of significance, the pills and the noisy space made it hard to concentrate on anything. She looked at Wellington and smiled cartoonishly, Wellington grinned back.

They turned to the new company introduced by Sensae for entertaining conversation. By now they'd had enough drinks and pills to talk to anyone. The talk was shouted loud enough for all to hear and became quite comedic, leading to waves of laughter for all. The laughs subsided while one of the chief jokers led Prudence on to the dance floor followed by others. Biscuit led Wellington. They laughed and danced and Ted Showbiz who had been on the dance floor all night greeted them all happily. They waved hello to Ted but those who knew him well made sure the strangers didn't get too close. Wellington was a terrible dancer, eventually he managed to excuse himself and return to a sitting position. Gertrude gave him a knowing look and laughed. The remaining dancers worked up quite a sweat and got close and sexy with Sensae's new friends. Upon returning to the table, at ten minutes to eleven O' clock, Biscuit quietly gave her contact details to Wellington.

At ten past twelve Prudence, Biscuit, Sensae, Gertrude, Wellington and Sensae's latest new attachments entered a venue serving consumables late into the evening. It was popular amongst the artists of the area, ensuring creative interpretations of the fashions at the time were on display amongst the patrons. This was a novelty for Wellington and his companions, who dressed for the most inside fashionable norms. This club was called *Yorkers*.

"I haven't been here before," Wellington remarked to Sensae.

"It's great. There's always a good vibe here and they have these black boxes that can talk to you," explained Sensae, a guiding hand on the robot's back. They found an appropriate and empty space to occupy and continued their discussion that had meandered along the company during the evening. Gertrude and Prudence went to purchase drinks for people and giggled at their own jokes on the way to a counter.

Conversation was interesting at *Yorkers*. Sensae would discuss his visits to flea markets with Wellington. Biscuit would talk about her shoes. Sensae's extra companions talked shoes with Biscuit, and how puffy their feet felt under the influence of whatever it was Sensae had supplied them with that evening. Gertrude and Prudence had taken some too and were glad to be walking more while fetching drinks. The other women were often standing up and switching seats with their friends to quench their puffy-feet restlessness. Gertrude and Prudence had gossiped about Sensae at the counter but stopped talking while they concentrated on not spilling the beverages for everyone.

The drinks were placed on a low-lying table and were snatched up by thirsty people. Prudence sat and switched seats with Sensae, who then switched with one of his new friends. Biscuit put her glass down and went over to Sensae to talk about the substance she was on and acknowledge her gratitude towards Sensae for introducing her to it. Prudence leaned towards one of Sensae's new friends and kissed them, then each of them got up to switch seats with somebody. When Wellington switched seats with one of them he sat next to a black box who tried to join in a conversation, prompting one with Wellington. There were no Telly-net monitors at *Yorkers* to distract Wellington from conversation, despite the stress the media was making of Yellow Orang-Utan Industries' business failures. This important subject, a concern for Wellington as a Yellow Orang-Utan employee, was diverted by the black box talker who happened to talk to Wellington and happened to talk about Peruvian nuns.

It was Biscuit who began to stare first. Biscuit was watching with big wide eyes, head bent toward a straw that helped her swallow her drink. Many of the party switched seats a bunch of times before noticing what Biscuit had. Gertrude's gaze joined Biscuit's and she said to Sensae, "what's Biscuit looking at?" Then she noticed what she was looking at.

"It's Wellington," Sensae replied, joining the growing stare. Wellington was deep in conversation with the black box talker. He had adjusted his body language to display his deliberate concentration. It limited him from interacting with the flesh people around him, unconsciously they had recognised his stance and hadn't asked to swap seats with him for several minutes, at least. He looked strangely strict and studious amongst his relaxed company. Soon they were all looking at him.

"And what about the lemon scented curtains?" Wellington asked the black box. His party began to listen to the conversation.

"Er-" answered the black box, uncharacteristically. Wellington continued his line of questioning, each question was reiterating a point he was making to counter a suggestion made by the black box. Eventually the black box gave in. Mouths hung open, they'd never seen a black box talking quite like this. Sensae began to laugh and it became contagious. Wellington and the black box was a unique comedy act, and it was inspiring. Everyone watched their discussion and burst into hoots of mirthful approval at regular short intervals, except Prudence and one of Sensae's attachments, still in each other's arms smooching and oblivious to the comedy. They stopped, looked at each other and sighed happily at eleven minutes past one.

By a quarter to two, Gertrude had led Wellington away from his new friends.

"You don't get drunk and you don't get sleepy," she remarked to her companion as they got nearer to the Yellow Orang-Utan Industries building.

"No," he answered. Gertrude was already beaming so she let out a chortle in reaction.

"I'm a bad dancer," he confessed.

"I noticed that, you're not coordinated that way I suppose."

"No," Wellington pursed his lips.

"You're not the only uncoordinated dancer in this city, you know."

"Well obviously not." The pair was now very near the entrance of the building that Wellington called home and Gertrude called work. Gertrude paused above an appropriate section of pavement and waited for Wellington to stop too. He noticed quickly and looked at her pretty face.

"I'm worried that Biscoe wants to have sex with you," Gertrude said carefully.

"I'm incapable of having sex with someone else," Wellington replied bluntly. "But how is Biscoe going to find that out? I mean, if she wants to have sex with you she's going to try and then you'll have to tell her." Gertrude bit her lower lip gently.

"Well I'll talk to Pepito about it, and see if that's OK. Biscoe did invite me to see her again, and this was what Pepi had in mind when we asked you to take me out. To socialise with your friends and make some of my own, develop a life outside the building behind us." Wellington explained. It was true, the building was behind them and they were very near the door. They farewelled and Gertrude included a friendly kiss upon Wellington's cheek at two O' clock in the morning.

14.

The houses looked so much alike that, time and time again, the kids went home by mistake to different houses and different families.

- One Flew Over The Cuckoo's Nest, 1962

The time was eleven O' four, it was eleven O' four and the president was impressed. He was reading reports somewhere in the vast expanse of the upper echelons of the Yellow Orang-Utan building. He was comfortable and warm and the reports were on paper. The accounting department produced the reports. The department produced more frequent reports lately. It was partly on the advice of Zabdiel Seinfeld, but also from the direction given by one of the Yellow Orang-Utan Industries' new executive board members. The new and frequent reports were also presented in a manner that better suited the real and fake corporation president. The president admired the graphs and the language of the reports. They told bad news, although this was presented well, which was what the president had enjoyed. It echoed the sentiment about his big company seen in the evening news and seemed to occasionally permeate the conditioned air of the famous building. Ever since Zabdiel Seinfeld had arrived things were turning from bad to worse, confirmed in part by the accounting department's reports. The president was getting used to this trend, which is why each consecutive report was less shocking. The good people of Yellow Orang-Utan Industries had been working harder and harder to regain their previously infallible market position. Defending themselves from the accusation that they may at some point desist being the biggest and most powerful corporation in the world. Claims like that had not been made for over a decade and back then, it had been Piano Smedley making them. Zabdiel was aiming them toward comparatively grim times.

"Gertrude, remind me to let the accounting department and related directors know that we're very pleased with their recent efforts," instructed the president.

"Yes sir," Gertrude replied, making a note of it. She went back to waiting for the president to sigh, imagining a game while she fought the boredom of watching an old man read. He still hadn't let out the rewarding exhalation at eleven twenty and six seconds.

At half past twelve Gertrude and the president ate lunch together. The president ate a slice of tapir meat with a spicy salad and Gertrude ate a small sandwich followed by an elegant bowl of chocolatey, nutty, ice cream. They had some music piped into the room.

"Don't forget to let the accounting department know that we're happy with their performance," reminded Gertrude between mouthfuls she found pleasantly smooth and creamy.

"Thank you, I won't" answered the president, pleased to be reminded and his thoughts returned to his work plans for the afternoon. The music shifted between tracks at twenty to one.

At fourteen minutes past four Biscuit popped her head into Wellington's office. Wellington wasn't in his office, he was behind Biscuit.

"Hallo Biscoe," he forwarded in his typically friendly way.

"Ooh, hi, there you are," Biscuit responded, quickly turning her head toward the sound of Wellington's voice.

"Are you here to remind me about our venture this evening?" He asked with a mockingly accusing tone.

"Yep," Biscuit replied playfully, with a grin. "We've only got a few hours of work left."

"That's very true, and I am really looking forward to our plans for the evening." He went into his office and Biscuit followed. He resumed his task at his workstation.

"Are you busy?" asked Biscuit.

"I'd say so, there's always something to be done here. Yellow Orang-Utan Industries isn't in good shape and needs assistance from everyone," answered Wellington with a firm yet cheery tone, he remained facing his workstation.

"Do you really think so? Last time I checked, Yellow Orang-Utan was still the biggest company in the world, buddy," Biscuit nonchalantly replied.

"Forgive me if I seem a bit paranoid, Biscoe. I just need to finish work, then I'll get changed and see you outside Stale Sun Screen tonight." Wellington finished, turning to face her.

"OK...I'll see you then. I'll go back to my boring office and see you tonight," echoed Biscuit obediently. She backed out of Wellington's office slowly, a grin matched by Wellingtons growing on her face. Wellington turned back to his workstation. It made sense to him to be concerned about the company he was created in. The bad news of Yellow Orang-Utan was on every night, but so was the good news, but other workers and departments didn't seem to use that information efficiently, Wellington wasn't one to speak up about it. The time was nineteen seconds to twenty past four.

After preparing a rushed dinner in her kitchen microwave, swallowing the last mouthful and putting on a jacket, Prudence was now riding to a pre-arranged rendezvous point at a quarter to eight, she was thinking of her friend Gertrude. On the way she used her cosmetic case to scan her face and purge it of spots and oils deemed disproportionate for her programmed settings, then remaining or resulting blemishes were spray-painted. With the majority of the travel out of the way Prudence shifted from the appropriate station, down the street and arrived at the pre-arranged rendezvous point. She didn't have to wait long. Gertrude arrived with a hurried step and slight puff and greeted Prudence.

Prudence was very tall, a lot of her implants had to be designed to accommodate her height. She had curly hair that she often wore up and made her look even taller. She had known Gertrude for a long time and was happy to see her again on this occasion, one in a countless series of adventures good and bad.

"Hello, Prudence," said Gertrude with a humorous tone.

"Hello Gertrude," Prudence replied with a matching tone, "it's a bit cold out here, we should go inside" she added. The details of this outing, the choice of movie and the venue, had been Prudence's idea. Gertrude agreed and the pair of friends ventured inside the cinema.

"What time's it start?" Gertrude asked.

"We'll see," Prudence answered confidently. When they did see, gazing up at the glowing board of available cinema session times, they realised they had some time to kill.

"Well in that case I'm going to buy some candy" Prudence declared and went about doing so. Gertrude followed her trusted companion. With sweets swallowed and digesting the two pretty women made another purchase and ventured into a dark room that their purchase had granted them access. Gertrude and Prudence sat for hours staring at a wall for a sophisticated light show with synchronous sound. The emotional impact on the pair was minimal, neither found cause to laugh, nor to bring them to tears. They walked out of the complex feeling the strain of keeping their eyeballs fixed in the same direction for too long.

"Well, that was a mistake," Prudence announced, then apologised to Gertrude for choosing a lacklustre show.

"It wasn't that bad," said Gertrude, a little sarcastically.

"Really? You think so?" asked Prudence.

"No," Gertrude answered with a smile. Prudence sighed grumpily.

"C'mon, lets go get a coffee." The pair moved from the building they had previously occupied to *Binary Nonsense*, a place that served coffee. The place served simple meals and other drinks too. It provided ordinariness to its satisfied, ordinary clientele. Its most outstanding feature was the loud, disturbing and iconoclastic art it hung on the walls, sometimes to the unannounced upset of first time visitors. In one corner a monitor played Telly-net that nobody paid attention to. Prudence sat with her back to it and let her hair down, Gertrude would occasionally glance at the monitor, but only to distract her from the ugly rendition of Piano Smedley that was among the loud, disturbing and iconoclastic décor. They also occasionally drank coffee, in sensible mouthfuls.

"So I think they're out tonight somewhere," reported Gertrude, on Biscuit and Wellington.

"Are you OK about that?" asked Prudence. Gertrude took a deep breath.

"There's stuff about him that Biscuit doesn't know," replied Gertrude, carefully.

"And you do know?" continued Prudence. Gertrude was swallowing coffee. She spent her time answering.

"I can't talk about it." Gertrude stirred her milky drink.

"Have you and he –" Prudence began.

"-No," Gertrude finished. Prudence was looking very worried.

"He won't do anything to her, he's not dangerous," said Gertrude trying to change Prudence's face, it did a little.

"It's just, he's...he's not someone you can get close to, like that," Gertrude stammered, deciding she'd already said too much.

"What? Is he gay?" Prudence's expression crept into outrageous excitement.

"No, no, nothing sexual." Gertrude said, smiling and furrowing her brow.

"Is he completely and devotedly in love with you?" continued Prudence.

"No!" Gertrude gladly changed the topic to Sensae's behaviour in the karaoke bar, *The Fabiola Chair*. She could do a hilarious impression of Sensae's pharmaceutically traumatised singing. At twelve minutes past eleven O' clock the coffee was gone and the table had to content itself with empty ceramics, creased serviettes, and two women singing terribly and guffawing heartily.

Wellington was waiting outside the *Stale Sun Screen* at eight thirty to see Biscuit there. After a few minutes Biscuit arrived with a similar hurried step and puffing breath that Gertrude had displayed to Prudence some minutes before in another part of the city.

"Hi Wellington," greeted Biscuit with a grin. She wore a colourful dress and a warm yet lightweight jacket. Wellington wore a collarless grey shirt, matching jacket and some jeans Pepito had purchased for Wellington especially for the occasion.

"Hallo Biscoe," returned Wellington, his grin mirroring hers in intensity.

"This place is great," she said leading him inside the *Stale Sun Screen*. The chequered, scribbled-on walls greeted Wellington's sensory input devices. There was a jukebox playing. It was biased towards old pop tunes and put to good use by the roller skating staff. Biscuit sniffed out a booth for them to spend over an hour occupying.

"Do they have vendors here?" asked Wellington, still being led by Biscuit's hand.

"Nope, it's all freshly prepared junk," replied the shorter of the two. They managed to sit themselves in a booth comfortably.

"Everybody writes poetry on the walls here," explained Biscuit, as Wellington read the messages there.

"Have you written any?" the robot asked.

"Somewhere, this place is open really late 'cause this street is surrounded by other late night clubs and stuff. So I've been here when I'm fairly wasted and I know I've written something but I can't remember what or where," Biscuit admitted.

"I suppose it would be rude to wander over everybody's tables while they're eating so you can try and jog your memory." Wellington said with a smile.

"Yes," agreed Biscuit, reading a touching scribble.

"Are you hungry?" asked Wellington.

"I think I'd like a drink first," Biscuit told Wellington. She craned her neck and widened her eyes to attract a waiter. Wellington copied her. Eventually someone skated up to their booth.

"Hello, are you guys ready to order?" the candy-pink outfitted servant inquired.

"Can I have a morose bible cider, please?" ordered Biscuit. Wellington read the waiter's name-tag, it indicated his name was Naphtali, and the tags were manufactured by the Dazzling Dimes company, based in Poland.

"And for you," continued the waiter's inquiry.

"Just a water for me, thanks" answered Wellington. The song changed on the jukebox. Wellington started to look at the bank of Telly-net monitors that were suspended from the ceiling, they could supply more information than the waiter's name-tag. Although Biscuit would share some stories over dinner and the poetry on the walls would be of some worthwhile scrutiny.

"What was your first visit here like?" Wellington said to prompt a story. Biscuit began giving a response, slowly as she jogged her memory for the episode, but then she got a grip on it and enhanced the drama without as many "ums" in the speech. Wellington reacted with more questions, to solicit wider context. Their drinks arrived before he'd recite a responding story he'd calculated.

The food was ordered and served and eating commenced. Their dinner at one point was interrupted when a gang of black-clad youths broke into an impromptu acapella rendition of one of their favourite songs, in defiance of one of the staff members' jukebox selection. The singers stood on their chairs and tables. The staff smiled, used to such behaviour. Other restaurant patrons smiled in appreciation of such deviance. Biscuit squealed in delight and clapped her hands, Wellington laughed. A few newcomers to the venue, who were without an experienced escort like Biscuit, weren't pleased and frowned discouragingly. When the chorus died down the patrons resumed eating, except for the singers who ran out into the street, one of them threatening a staff member, not Naphtali, but the one who picked the song. The recipient staff member blew the customer a raspberry and gave him the finger, they were both friends.

"I've seen stuff like that happen here before," commented Biscuit gleefully.

After the secretary and her robotic man companion had eaten dinner, Biscuit addressed Wellington's habit of being occasionally distracted by the Telly-net monitors.

"I'm sorry Biscuit, but I work in market hacking at Yellow Orang-Utan and I'm obliged to process a lot of market related news to improve my work performance." Wellington tried to explain. Biscuit reached across the table and took hold of Wellington's hands. He leaned in a little himself to make the gesture easier.

"Please, do not talk about work. I don't find it engaging or interesting, I just work there OK. I'm just a secretary." Biscuit said, slowly, but not too seriously.

"Biscuit, don't take Yellow Orang-Utan Industries for granted. It can't be the biggest corporation in the world forever, everything changes." Wellington said convincingly.

"I think we should pay the bill and then I'll take you to another place across the street," said Biscuit. They paid the bill. Wellington looked at something on the monitors along the way.

"I'm going to tell you all about my work when we're across the street," threatened Wellington in a hushed tone, while Biscuit was being handed back her credit card and spieled at by a *Stale Sun Screen* servant. The time was nine fifty-one and twenty seconds.

At ten O' three the president was washing his hands after using the toilet when he heard the phone ring and he rushed as fast as his feeble old body could manage, to answer it.

"Hello?" he answered unexpectedly.

"Hi Arty," said the phone receiver. His hearing was working fine, the president recognised the voice of Magnum Ndgali.

"Hi Magnum," the president said to the voice. He was thinking back to when he'd last seen Magnum, he guessed it would have been in the Swinging Hanky a week or so prior to this phone call. What had happened in between? He egged on Magnum for his lecherous tales of sexual conquests to give him more time to think. His private guesswork kept his mind off Magnum's tales of women, money and power, and away from reminders about his failing member that the tales normally provoked.

"But I'm getting distracted," directed Magnum, after a hearty laugh led to a wet coughing fit.

"Oh?" exclaimed the president smoothly, clearly losing his private guessing game.

"Arty, my co-conspirators are pressuring me to withdraw our attentions, financial and otherwise, from Yellow Orang-Utan Industries." Magnum Ndgali spoke carefully.

"Uh huh," replied the president, he wanted to laugh, but he knew any laughter that would come out of him would sound nervous.

"I don't want to turn my back on you Arty, Yellow Orang-Utan has changed life as we know it and I'm glad to have been a major part of it as early on as I did. But, but I watch the news Arty, I know you've been watching it too. And it's not looking good, speculation is that your tower is about to fall." The president could hear the sound of heavy breaths through the telephone earpiece in his room.

"Heck, they've been saying that on and off for years," replied the president.

"I know, I know, that's what I've been telling my board too. But they're not content to accept that story. If you'd spend more time with us at the *Hanky* you'd hear that mine's not the only board saying so either. There's something moving, something changing," Magnum said with an invisible pout. "If I side with you against better opinion it may be curtains for me too."

"It's Zabdiel Seinfeld, isn't it?" suggested the Yellow Orang-Utan Industries president.

"Of course it is." The air around the old corporate men grew cold despite the conditioning.

"If I could be coy, sit tight my friend, he may just have a few surprises yet. Have I ever let you down before?" bluffed the president.

"No, Arty. You better not be bluffing. I think I like your answer whether you're bluffing or not, but you better not be. I can't ignore the better judgement of my peers and my company for much longer." The phone trembled in the president's hand.

"Relax Magnum, I'm fine here and you should be over there. Sure there's Seinfeld here, but Seinfeld's got Yellow Orang-Utan here and he hasn't even begun to wield that." He began to feel weak at the knees.

"I'm getting too old for this," said Magnum.

"Me too."

"Yeah, but you're still a dog, Arty." With that farewell, the telephonic connection ceased and the president of Yellow Orang-Utan Industries was more acutely aware of how alone in his room he was. He wondered if there was still time to catch some fresh bad news on the Telly-net, the time was quarter past ten.

"So the rate of hippopotami attacks affects the price of pretzel dough?" Biscuit suggested at seventeen minutes past eleven. She didn't quite understand, and not sure she ever would, but Wellington's explanation was at least mildly entertaining.

"Very indirectly and yet very significantly," the robot agreed. He sipped a tea Biscuit had ordered for him.

"If Yellow Orang-Utan Industries ended its association with Dinosaurs R Us the whole connection between them would end and the market would react dramatically," summarised Wellington. Incense smoke wafted around the pair.

"Are you sure this works and you haven't gone insane?" asked Biscuit.

"That would be impossible. I'm telling you if the company cuts its ties with Dinosaurs R US, the very next night the Yellow Orang-Utan board of directors will have a glowing reception on the news." Wellington came across as enthusiastic and confident.

"So we'd have to sell off the shares in the dinosaur company?" asked Biscuit.

"Dinosaurs R Us, yes," corrected Wellington.

"But how do you know this?" Biscuit didn't care too much. He was nuts, he was bonkers, but there wasn't an awkward silence to be had in this conversation.

"The way the hippo attack on the Telly-net site looked just then. It involves a good grasp of media representation, audience reaction and how that relates to the stock market. That's all hacking is, finding the connections between the various elements that make up the modern world and capitalising on it in the business sector. It's financial fashion." The pair both sipped their drinks. Biscuit, relaxing with Wellington and a coffee, let her hair down.

"With the little power I have in the market hacking department, I try to bend other hackers' behaviour towards the trend I can predict, but nobody seems to follow. They're going in the same tired direction and it's having negative ramifications in the market and the media. With Zabdiel Seinfeld and the new board of directors making the executive decisions, it's making it even worse. Yellow Orang-Utan is close to great losses." Wellington hung his head trying to look appropriately sad.

"I'm sure you're doing your work well enough to get noticed eventually. If you're right, they'll notice your success compared to their failure, won't they?" Biscuit said encouragingly, patting Wellington on the knee.

"Maybe, I'll talk to my boss," Wellington said. He straightened his posture and looked at Biscuit.

"I'm sorry, I won't talk about work anymore. You didn't want to talk about work and I forced it on you. Sorry if I talked too much," apologised the polite robot.

"That's OK, a conversation as crazy as yours can be pretty amusing," said Biscuit, grinning with lips moist from coffee sips. Relaxed and with a warm, full belly, she was content not to talk anymore. Wellington felt no such sensations when the time was eleven thirty.

At five minutes to midnight one woman and a robot walked along the street that contained Biscuit's house. A taxi had delivered them to the street and Wellington would continue to ride in the taxi in about five minutes. They walked closely together, occasionally parts of Biscuit's anatomy would brush against Wellington softly.

"Wellington," Biscuit was heard to say. She had stopped and looked up at him.

"Yes Biscoe?" Wellington replied.

"Will you sleep with me tonight?" Biscuit asked. Biscuit held Wellington's hand. She kissed his lubricated and electrically warmed lips, he approximated a politely warm response, holding her waist.

"Um?" said Biscuit, looking hopefully at Wellington.

"Biscoe, I'm sorry, but I'm a robot. I can't sleep...with, anybody." Wellington said, carefully.

"Oh, good bye then, I hope you had a good time." Biscuit said with a very friendly tone, she let go of Wellington's hand, reacting automatically to the rejection before the words had registered in her mind.

"Goodbye Biscoe, I did have a good time and I'll talk to you again very soon," Wellington said, proceeding slowly to the taxi. He got in the taxi and rode away, waving at Biscuit. Biscuit watched the taxi disappear from view and stood, stuck outside her house.

"Um", Biscuit said, fidgeting with her key, distracted by a rising heat in her head. It was midnight.

15.

Girls experience their first menstrual period towards the end of puberty and boys find they can ejaculate.

- Biology: A Functional Approach, 1986

Biscuit ceased her stride across the ground floor foyer of the Yellow Orang-Utan Industries building, and at six O' nine remained paused, legs together in one spot. Wellington remained paused on his spot of the foyer. The foyer was of marvellous architecture and a highlight of the tour available for tourists visiting the biggest building in the world. She started towards the elevator that she could ride towards work.

"Biscoe," called Wellington calmly.

"What?" she called back crossly. He joined her in the elevator with a handful of other Yellow Orang-Utan Industries employees, and visitors. There they said nothing while the other passengers imagined what they would be saying once they got out of the elevator. Each became silently upset as they alighted on lower levels and the imaginary gossipy showdown between the two was enacted itself in corridors above, or forgotten about.

"We have to discuss further the information I gave you last night," the robot said.

"Should I really bother?" asked Biscuit, not yet believing Wellington was what he had claimed to be.

"My superiors insist they talk to you. Only they, yourself, and Gertrude know about this," said Wellington.

"That you're a robot?" Biscuit asked sarcastically. Wellington used body language to encourage a discreet, hushed conversation.

"Yes." Biscuit pulled Wellington into a toilet nearby.

"Prove it," she said staring up at him with a furrowed brow.

"Perhaps if there's a part during the working day when you get bored and are free, like yesterday when you visited me at my office. Perhaps then would be a good time to meet with my superiors and I can explain," suggested Wellington.

"I want you to show me how you're a robot," she demanded.

"What do you want me to show?" asked the robot.

"Bits, I want to see some robot bits, some wires coming out of your chest or something. Take off your shirt," instructed Biscuit. Wellington began unbuttoning his shirt. With the buttons undone, Biscuit pulled open a shirt to see anatomical anomalies not seen on humans. This wasn't enough for Biscuit, the secretary from Yellow Orang-Utan Industries continued searching her fellow employees' body until she found sufficient proof they were a robot.

"OK, you're a robot," said a satisfied but suddenly foolish-feeling

Biscuit.

"Will you please meet with my superiors to discuss this? Gertrude can be with us when we do if she has the available time," the robot pleaded.

"I guess," Biscuit conceded.

"Thank you Biscoe, I will try to explain things well and amusingly then."

Wellington, now returned to a presentable appearance for a robot, made his way out of the toilet and towards his office in the market hacking department of the company building. Biscuit stayed in the toilet for a while, now aware that what she'd heard last night was not the worst excuse ever, she really had tried to get a robot to sleep with her. At nine nineteen, she swore then inhaled quickly and a tear formed on her cheek.

Gertrude excused herself from lunch with the president of Yellow Orang-Utan Industries at twenty to one and journeyed to lower echelons of the big building to find Biscuit. She grabbed a cup of noodles from a vendor on the way. She found her poorly looking friend in a large dining area.

"He's a robot," said Biscoe, when Gertrude had sat down and looked her friend in the eyes.

"Wellington? Yes. You didn't -?" Gertrude began, not expecting to finish.

"I tried," whimpered Biscuit. Gertrude moaned sympathetically and moved closer to Biscuit. Then she opened her lunch's packaging.

"It's supposed to be a secret. He and Pepito asked me to take him out of the building and introduce him to people. I'm sorry Biscoe." Biscuit sipped on a large smoothie.

"He kissed me, well, I kissed him," she admitted. Gertrude's eyes widened slightly. She bit into the green noodles on her chopsticks. "Was that OK?" Gertrude asked.

"I guess, it seemed OK at the time. But then I found out," replied Biscuit, she paused while Gertrude swallowed, "who's Pepito?"

"He's the guy that made Wellington, he works in the computer lab." Gertrude looked at her sad friend, Biscuit looked so weak and defeated, she had been recently teary.

"He wants to meet after work in the computer lab," said Biscuit.

"He has a room there with lots of computers and TV screens and Wellington spends a lot of time there," explained Gertrude, "I had to go there when they told me all about him."

"Did they tell you all about the stock market?" asked Biscuit. "No, they talked about a whole bunch of other confusing stuff though." Gertrude fished some more noodles out of her cup. Biscuit stirred her smoothie with its complementary straw.

"He was telling me all about the market last night, all this weird stuff, he sounded nuts," Biscuit said after a sip.

"If I had a computer for a brain, I'd sound nuts as well," Gertrude retorted.

"You'll get over it," Gertrude said reassuringly, "I mean, you got over Piano, didn't you?" Biscuit hunched over her smoothie and sighed.

"I guess enough time has passed for me to put it out of my mind. It makes the new guy seem pretty annoying though, it's not the same without Piano."

"It's not, and the company's not doing very well," Gertrude paused, "now that I know about Wellington, since I found out, I've liked him a lot more than before, so I think you'll get over it."

"Well I hope so," replied Biscuit. "Is the company really in that bad a shape?"

"Things are pretty dim upstairs," Gertrude answered before attacking her cup of noodles again.

"Wellington was talking about this Dinosaurs 'R' Us company, he said if we stopped investing in them, um, we'd get better or something," announced Biscuit quietly, staring up at Gertrude, who looked up at Biscuit from her lunch.

"Really?" Gertrude asked with her mouthful.

"That was something he tried to make very clear when he was blathering about the stock market last night," Biscuit didn't know what it meant, but she was happy to have remembered. The time was ten past one.

At ten to two, the president had finished his lunch in his private boardroom and moved to his more frequently visited room where he finished reading a report he had begun that morning. It was also the time when Gertrude returned to her task of minding the old man's business and personal affairs.

"Gertrude, could you please have a cleaner sent to the board room?" the president asked without looking up from his reading.

"Yes, sir," she answered quickly. She went to a nearby communications console and communicated a message to a cleaner. With that task complete, Gertrude looked around for her clipboard, found it, and sat around waiting for the president of Yellow Orang-Utan Industries to give her more instructions. Today the president was wearing a grey shirt and a black suit and was comfortable and familiar with the clothes. Gertrude wore a white dress with a generous split up the leg and a light jacket of a blue grey appearance.

When the president finished his report he gave the document to Gertrude to file away or destroy, depending on the type of document, and Gertrude left with the document to visit the appropriate room to process it accordingly. He then meandered over to a desk and fiddled with his computer and its software to begin a scheduled call to the vice presidents of Yellow Orang-Utan Industries. He'd learned of the scheduled call from Gertrude that morning, she had it marked on her clipboard. Gertrude returned to the room when the dial tone could be heard on speakers around the president's room. The shrill ring echoed around the room very briefly before it was answered by one of the vice presidents.

"Hello?" said a voice pertaining to Letitia Bjorksdotter. The president replied to the voice. Gertrude didn't see his lips move, she heard the voice of Zabdiel Seinfeld. Zabdiel handled the whole conference call between him, vice president Letitia Bjorksdotter and vice president Naamah Nelise while a biological president sat in listening without speaking himself. Zabdiel, Naamah and Letitia discussed ways to improve business but the answers weren't coming quickly enough for all to be satisfied. The president assumed his customary frown as he continued to listen.

Gertrude drifted in and out of concentration to the phone call. Then she remembered from her earlier conversation with Biscuit, just as Biscuit had from her conversation with Wellington, the suggestion that ending company investment in Dinosaurs 'R' Us would be somehow beneficial to the company, her eyes widened. She listened more carefully to the phone conversation playing on the speakers.

After the phone call ended the president of Yellow Orang-Utan Industries let out a relaxed sigh.

"Um, a friend of mine gave me an investment tip about Yellow Orang-Utan Industries," Gertrude began.

"What?" asked the president, knowing already what she said. Gertrude repeated her conversation prompt but the president interrupted her.

"What kind of tip?" he asked.

"Well, they said Yellow Orang-Utan should sell off something called Dinosaurs 'R' Us," Gertrude said awkwardly.

"Who told you that?" asked the president.

"A friend," replied Gertrude.

"Does he work here?" asked the president, presuming a 'he'.

"Yes, yes they do."

"In market hacking? We have a huge department of the company dedicated to following the stock market and balancing our investments for optimum performance. That sort of thing is almost the overriding function of the company, almost," began the president: "If this tip is useful I'm sure he could make the right investment choices with it, it's his job after all." The president hadn't taken his eyes away from his boring screen the whole time he talked to Gertrude.

"I suppose you're right," Gertrude conceded. She bent down in her chair, placed her hands on her chin and scowled. Today she wore her hair up and the buttons on her dress were pink. The time was forty-three minutes past two, seventeen minutes to three.

At four forty-four Wellington saw Gertrude enter the room in the information technology laboratory that was kept locked and entry available only to him and Pepito, who he called Pepi. Wellington was already inside, as was Pepito, and Biscuit. She greeted Pepito, who had opened the door for her, before quickly turning towards Biscuit.

"Hi, is everything OK?" she inquired of her friend.

"So far," her friend answered. Biscuit was holding a large cup of coffee. So was Pepito.

"Coffee?" offered Pepito. There was another cup placed on a familiar orthopaedic wooden object next to Biscuit's matching chair. Gertrude took the coffee graciously without a word and sat next to Biscuit.

"We've just apologised to Biscoe for ah, betraying her trust," explained Pepito. Biscuit had visited Wellington in his office and said she was ready to meet with his superiors. Wellington made a call to Pepito then escorted Biscuit between storeys of the building and to this room in the computer lab. She met Pepito, who immediately apologised earnestly and offered to answer any questions she had.

"Would you like to know how I work, it's something we told Gertrude," offered Wellington.

"No," said Biscuit, she sipped her coffee.

"How have you been, Gertrude?" asked Wellington.

"I've been reasonably well," replied Gertrude, she wanted to be on Biscuit's side of the situation but had been enjoying Wellington's company more and more. Pepito looked into Biscuit's downcast gaze.

"What would you like to know, Biscoe?" he asked. Biscuit took another sip from her coffee. She swallowed the sip.

"Well," she began, "um, I think all I really wanted was an apology."

"I've apologised and Wellington has apologised too," explained Pepito, trying not to sound too defensive.

"Mmm, yeah, but...I just don't think it should have to happen to anyone else. It wasn't much fun, you know. I don't think Wellington should keep secrets like that," said Biscuit.

"Hmmm," said Pepito, thinking out loud, "I don't know about that."

"Why not?" demanded Biscuit, although keeping her tone quiet. Gertrude watched Pepito's face carefully.

"Well, if he's working for Yellow Orang-Utan Industries and if everyone is to know he's a robot, he might lose his job. I mean if he tells anyone there has to be an explanation, like the two of you," said Pepito, throwing a gesture toward the female pair.

"And a lot of these questions lead back to me, I made him using company resources, without authorisation, and I don't want to get into trouble." The female pair watched Pepito's brief attempt at a cute pout. Biscuit viewed through narrowed eye slits.

"People have difficulty interacting with common robots and I'm a robot of unique design and programming, it may be they'd discover me with shock and disbelief, " offered Wellington. Pepito looked at him sternly.

"I didn't believe," added Gertrude.

"Neither did I, and I was upset," seconded Biscuit, who still was a bit, although it was being engulfed by confusion.

"Wellington, perhaps it would be better to keep your interactions outside the building to a minimum. We've kept a low profile inside, and I suppose we may cause less upset if we do the same outside. I mean Gertrude was only the first person to suspect you in here, but if you keep advancing yourself socially outside, there will be more people becoming suspicious," suggested Pepito.

"I think that no matter who finds out, they're owed an apology and an explanation and the less we have of those the less people have been upset. I think it would work out better that way," Pepito finished with a sigh, hoping that was a sufficient argument for the small secretary.

"You should be accountable for your actions," said an unsatisfied Biscuit.

"Originally we agreed to let me out of the building to test whether or not I could pass as human in a more social environment," said Wellington, "perhaps the test is over."

"I agree with you Wellington," said Pepito, initially ignoring Biscuit.

"There's still a problem, what about all of Gertrude's and my friends? They'll find out Wellington's a robot eventually, shouldn't you sit down and explain this stuff to them too?" exclaimed Biscuit.

"Not necessarily, and not if we can help it," answered Pepito sternly. Biscuit audibly huffed.

"I think he's right," Gertrude said assuredly, "I don't think our friends will find out quite like you did, Biscoe. Wellington volunteered his true story to me when I demanded an explanation for him being here in the lab."

"You should be accountable to my friends for Wellington," repeated Biscuit.

"Well if they find out he's a robot, certainly. But keeping Wellington's robot secret is still as important as before," answered Pepito, "if the wrong kind of person finds out I'll get in trouble, and that's probably not important to you. But what would happen to Wellington if he got found out by the wrong person?" The three humans looked at the robot.

"OK, fine," was all she had to say before someone else happily changed the subject and the chatter became more comfortable and flowing. Gertrude asked Wellington about the stock market oddity Biscuit had mentioned. He began to explain while Pepito probed him about it further. When all the coffee was gone people decided they should stand, leave the room and return to their final duties on their working day at Yellow Orang-Utan Industries. Wellington opened the door for them all. Three of them bid Pepito farewell as he returned to his office and made their way to the entrance of the information technology laboratory, where a security guard let them through at exactly fifteen minutes past five.

The time was nineteen minutes past five. The president was at the end of his working day, mostly because the sun was in the process of setting, the work never exactly stopped for the president of Yellow Orang-Utan Industries. He was waiting for Gertrude to return to his room. She did in less than a minute. She greeted him and discussed with him his immediate thoughts on evening wear, she left his company again then returned with suitable garments for the president's dinner at *The Swinging Hanky*. He began to undress in front of his assistant and she helped him into the elegant suit. She fastened his green buttons. His suit looked fine, he had an ugly wrinkly face sticking out of it, but that was an unfortunate necessity. He was ready for a dinner outing. He thanked Gertrude and bid her farewell for that day, expecting to see her the following morning. Gertrude bowed politely then picked up her clipboard then left the president's company and the Yellow Orang-Utan building.

The President waited patiently in his room for the familiar phone call from Windle. Windle's call indicated to the president that he'd arrived at his post and was ready to meet the president's wishes. The president greeted him warmly. He had Windle arrange an automotive escort for his trip to *The Swinging Hanky*. Shortly after the phone call the president made his way down to the ground floor of the building to meet the escort. On the way he examined his appearance in a mirror. He'd changed from one suit to another, but they were all mostly the same, in function and character. The mirror was full length, his appearance didn't impress him and he didn't gaze for very long. When he stepped out of the elevator on the ground floor he made his way out of the building, watched by eyes of security guards and displayed on monitors to even more security guards.

He rode through the city to another building, one he didn't live in. He walked through the ground floor of that one and into another elevator. He rode it to the floor that was known to many as *The Swinging Hanky* restaurant. The brightly lit space dazzled many as they entered. The polished metallic fixtures that adorned most of the furnishings inside added to the glare. The president of Yellow Orang-utan Industries was accustomed to it. He was accustomed to the staff that greeted him immediately upon entering, they would also escort him to his customary seat. He thanked them and perused the familiar menu. The familiar voices reverberated across his ears, the drunkard wife and the permanent resident, always there like the furniture. He would hear the collection of phone ring tones and their wealthy masters hatching their business. If he applied himself he very well may have been able to identify them all by their busy phones ringing during their dinners. He didn't apply himself. He barely spoke to them, even though all were frequent visitors to this restaurant.

Magnum Ndgali was different. He often spoke to many of them and called them all Arty. He entered *The Swinging Hanky* with a group of his company associates then quietly sat with them around their table. The Yellow Orang-Utan president noticed them and sipped a glass of water brought by a waiter when he ordered his dinner. The performance of Yellow Orang-Uan of late hadn't dramatically improved since Ndgali had phoned the president personally and asked for clues concerning the continuing strength of the company. The group assembled around that large table spoke despondently without hints of laughter. When his party had entered, the whole chatter of the room had calmed, imperceptible to many, due to chewing and phone calls. The president's food arrived. He ate his dinner quietly, there wasn't anyone dining with him to talk to, and his meal allowed small, polite bites. Magnum Ndgali made eye contact with the president of Yellow Orang-Utan Industries, and there was no change of expression,

Magnum was frowning, made plainer by the arrangement of his facial hair. The president looked down at the nearest tablecloth.

At *The Swinging Hanky*, the restaurant's peak dining period was drawing to a close. The president had nearly finished his dessert, which he was eating very slowly. Magnum was talking to a business associate at another table. He had quietly greeted a few other diners about the restaurant while his company associates finished their meals and prepared to leave. He returned to their table when half of them had left, just as half the restaurant visitors had left. He had not greeted the Yellow Orang-Utan president. The president was sure of this because he was now paying close attention to the behaviour and movements of Magnum Ndgali. Magnum stood with the remaining company fellows and moved towards the exit. He did look back sternly at the president. The president leant back in his chair and raised his eyebrows at him good-humouredly. At twenty-five minutes to eight, he slumped back forward.

16.

And they started spreading by themselves like they were going to snap off my body, and I thought I'm going to die this way, and how will anyone understand that I tried to keep my legs closed, but they burned and I couldn't.

- The Secret Diary of Laura Palmer, 1990

At ten past twelve Gertrude stifled a giggle. She was on the phone with Biscuit at lunchtime. The president of Yellow Orang-Utan Industries sat in his private boardroom. Gertrude, who had been dining in there previously, had dashed out when she got the call. She squatted down and against a wall.

"Alright," agreed Gertrude into the mouthpiece.

"Excellent," declared Biscuit. They both spoke between mouthfuls of lunch.

"What floor are you going to be on?" asked Gertrude. Biscuit told her of her future whereabouts. Gertrude listened carefully, making a pause in her chewing.

"OK, I'll see you then, hey-" whispered Gertrude, knowing that the president may hear her hatching plans to skimp on her duty to him that afternoon. She and Biscuit continued to exchange small talk for a few more minutes over their phone connection, pausing to eat giggle or swallow. Then they both agreed to terminate the connection. Gertrude stood up straight and re-joined the president to finish their lunch. He'd been ordering noodles in a cup all week long. The time was thirteen minutes past twelve and ten seconds.

The time was thirty-five minutes past one. Gertrude scurried out of the elevator and down what she hoped was the right corridor. She was looking for the very large meeting room where the entire Yellow Orang-Utan PR department were having a very large meeting. Zabdiel Seinfeld had fired the PR people who had opted to capitalise on the death of Piano Smedley, like he'd done with the old board of executive directors. The new board of executive directors were hiring new PR people. A few members of the board of executive directors were present at the meeting too. Biscuit found Gertrude quickly as she entered the busy, noisy room.

"Hello," she whispered under the din.

"Hello Biscoe," Gertrude whispered back. They found a discreet place in the very big room away from the PR types' ruckus. They figured this meeting was a waste of their time. They continued to whisper amongst themselves so as not to appear to be contributing to the meeting.

"I told the president about Dinosaurs 'R' Us. He said Wellington could do the right thing with it himself," said Gertrude.

"He can't. He keeps trying but there's restricted access to that stuff. It might be why he told us about it," responded Biscuit. The pair watched the PR people bark at each other with their shrill voices, it was a sensible meeting but incoherent to the women whispering.

"He's pretty funny when he talks about the stock market though, like when he was talking to the black boxes at Yorkers," said Biscuit.

"And what about the lemon scented curtains?" imitated Gertrude. They both grinned and laughed inwardly.

"Too bad he's a robot," added Biscuit with a little sigh.

"I know what you mean," Gertrude added between pursed lips, "he's quite the gentleman."

"Have you ever thought about it?" asked Biscuit.

"A while ago," answered Gertrude.

"If only," breathed Biscuit playfully. They were both grinning. They watched the PR types try to fit their personalities, tempers and emotions inside the decorum of corporate meeting structures.

"You'd think there would've been something that would give it away," Biscuit ventured.

"What do you mean?" asked Gertrude.

"His robot-ty-ness, you'd think there'd be more to passing as human," suggested Biscuit.

"Well, men and women pass as each other all the time," responded Gertrude," and I'm sure Pepi knew enough about it to be thorough when he made him. He looks real."

"But when I kissed him...He even tasted real. His skin felt normal, he even smelt right," confessed Biscuit. Gertrude lifted her arm and exposed her armpit to Biscuit.

"Hello Biscoe, perfume implants, nobody smells normal anymore," she said, "Wellington probably hasn't got anything your average catwalk model wouldn't have in the cosmetic department. Wellington would make a good model, actually. We should make him the Yellow Orang-Utan poster boy."

"Wellington's better than that," said Biscuit disapprovingly. Gertrude sighed.

"You're right," she conceded, then playfully added, "are you sure he's a robot?"

"Yes, he's definitely a robot," said Biscuit at thirteen minutes to two.

"Too bad."

"Yeah, too bad."

Later that evening it was fifteen minutes past ten. The president of Yellow Orang-Utan Industries was in bed watching Telly-net. He was watching a satirical comedy show. He wasn't laughing. Before he watched the comedy he watched, out of obligation to his company, news media reporting on the failings of Yellow Orang-Utan Industries. Then his telephone rang. He eagerly shifted to answer the call from his phone console.

"Hello?" he said into the mouthpiece.

"Arty, we've been old friends..." came an abrupt voice through the phone.

"Magnum? Hi," began the president of Yellow Orang-Utan Industries.

"...So I'll be up front. Do you want to hear about the girl who blew me with a mouthful of glitter or do you want to hear about the meeting you're having with my lawyers to negotiate my company's withdrawal of financial investment in Yellow Orang-Utan Industries?"

The Yellow Orang-Utan president paused when he heard Magnum Ndgali's offer.

"Oh," he eventually said, "I'm sorry, Magnum."

"Will you fight this?" asked Magnum.

"With our lawyers and your lawyers it could be a very sporting affair," suggested the president.

"True," admitted Magnum, "and that's what they'll want to do, we can let them play for a while."

"But I suppose this is what your board wants you to do, and eventually people do what they want regardless of contracts."

"Don't be so despondent, Arty. You've disappointed me enough as it is."

"I suppose this is a unique opportunity for Zabdiel Seinfeld," mused the president. "Piano faced a crisis or two and was all the better for it."

"What are you saying, Arty? You always get so coy when you talk about your proxies, let me tell you about the glitter-girl," wrangled Magnum through the phone.

"Desperate times, Magnum. I could be bluffing but honestly, I don't have anything. Piano was the only good thing going at this place. There isn't a soul left on the planet that hasn't been changed by the innovations instituted by Yellow Orang-Utan. We exhausted the need for the revolution we'd pioneered. It's investments, stocks and our power base that's perpetuated us for the last decade. The core of Yellow Orang-Utan Industries obeyed the law of physics long ago and slowed down. It was the cult of personality around Piano Smedley that kept the Yellow Orang-Utan alive on the perpetual motion machine of the global economy." The president was defeated and felt incoherent and desperate. He masked it under the veneer of a lying old man.

"Don't gimme that physics balderdash. Everybody needs their trinkets, they always have and always will. Everybody's pathetic little desires don't obey the laws of physics," said Magnum, glad now he'd blanked this president at the Swinging Hanky.

"Losing you is going to throw Zabdiel out of his comfort zone, he'll be forced to eat, sleep, and think outside the square we've been nurturing him in. It's probably what we should have done a lot earlier. It'll be character defining. It's what we've been waiting for. You wouldn't believe me if I said that we need your company to withdraw your investment in order to have Zabdiel blossom into the leader we designed him to be, would you?"

"No, I think you're all out of coy. My personal stock will remain with Yellow Orang-Utan Industries, I'm loyal to the end – plus I wouldn't know where the hell I filed the paperwork for it. But my company will begin withdrawal procedures for the company stock tomorrow." The president felt thirsty and confused. He ended the phone conversation diplomatically.

"Goodbye, Arty," was the last thing Magnum Ndgali was heard to say via phone. The president fetched himself a drink of water, then made one call to Windle, delegating a memo.

"Could you please report this to the relevant departments? I trust your discretion to tell the right people," he said.

"Certainly sir," said Windle with his evergreen pleasantness.

"Thanks, Windle," sighed the president. The president, finished with his phone for a while, shifted back into his bed and turned off the muted Wall-span.

He crawled inside his bedclothes and tried to sleep. He had moderate success. He lay awake feeling desperate and afraid. It was an inspiring moment. Now he felt real fear, he was sweaty in places, his penis he was sure had disappeared inside him entirely, and he was seriously thinking about the benefits of sucking his thumb. Eventually the president got to sleep. But it wasn't too restorative or deep. He got up again at one point to ring Windle.

"Windle?" called the president, once appropriate beeps indicated the open communication line.

"Yes sir?" said Windle invitingly.

"Please see to it that Yellow Orang-Utan Industries sells its way out of involvement with the company called Dinosaurs 'R' Us."

Then it was still very dark as the time was two thirty-six and twenty-four seconds in the morning.

17.

Led by the blind, into ditches
Or chasing their own tails like bitches
Seduced by power and lust for riches.

- The Katha Upanishad, 2:5

At ten thirty in the morning, Gertrude wasn't paying attention to the Wall-span TV, which was a shame. The president had watched the breaking financial news with more attentiveness. It could be because Gertrude had arranged a healthy nutritious breakfast for the president of Yellow Orang-Utan Industries, whereas Gertrude, in her haste to be at work in time to arrange breakfast for someone else, had wolfed down snack foods and a pill or two for breakfast. The president was aware that below him there were two teams of lawyers negotiating investment contracts that involved the largest investment in the largest corporation in the world. This was possibly the most important case the lawyers would ever handle, and they had to fight that case while containing their excitement and not losing their cool. And pieces of information were slowly leaked out to the media and being reported throughout the world.

Between approximately ten forty-five and eleven O' clock that morning the story was reported concerning the recently sold company Dinosaurs 'R' Us. It was reported in a more light-hearted matter than the story of the alleged rift between Zabdiel Seinfeld and Magnum Ndgali's respectful companies. It came across as a diamond in Yellow Orang-Utan Industries' rough. The story was told visually with a cheering crowd of workers, a man in a suit shaking hands with and presenting a briefcase to a weak man in a hospital bed, and a panda bear sleeping next to a llama. It was said, in relation to this affair, via the vast communication network of Telly-net, that Zabdiel Seinfeld had put one foot right that morning.

The Yellow Orang-Utan newsfeed droned on and on, the president sipped a coffee and Gertrude thought about what she'd drink at her outing to Fishpaste that evening, as it reached one minute past twelve in the noon.

At thirteen minutes past one Pepito was eating his lunch in a nondescript luncheon area of the Yellow Orang-Utan building. Lately, this area had not been very full during the periods people claimed for their lunch, many were too concerned about their jobs and futures with Yellow Orang-Utan to make social development a lunchtime priority. But this was why Pepito had chosen to eat here, it was quiet. Wellington appeared and sat with him.

"Hello," greeted Pepito amongst a mouthful of hamburger.

"Hallo Pepi," Wellington returned, before heading to the lunch bar to get himself a hamburger.

"Yellow Orang-Utan sold Dinosaurs 'R' Us today," Wellington said once seated with Pepito. He placed his lunch order on their table. It was identical to Pepito's according to Wellington's social protocols.

"How did you do that?" asked Pepito.

"I didn't, I guess we just told the right people. Eventually the idea was spread to someone with power enough to make the necessary arrangements."

"And it's made the news," Pepito replied. "That's not good for a low profile, Wellington."

"But it is good for Yellow Orang-Utan Industries. Anyhow, I didn't do it," the robot protested.

"But you knew about it," Pepito swallowed, "what can you do now that it's sold off?"

"There were some things I could do to capitalise on this change and I exacted them this morning at work," answered Wellington.

"Do these things relate to the devaluation of Yellow Orang-Utan stock and the lawyers negotiating a very important investment contract today?" asked Pepito.

"Of course, we're going to lose that fight," Wellington replied after politely finishing his mouthful.

"Really? You're sure?" Pepito narrowed his eyes. Wellington nodded.

"Very well. There's some kangaroo in this burger," Pepito

remarked.

"Mmm, I prefer it in sausages," lied Wellington. Pepito marvelled at the lie. Wellington was designed to say that; he'd never eaten kangaroo sausages. He'd never eaten. Pepito would collect a plastic bag full of mushed up food from inside Wellington at the end of the day. He watched the robot's messy hair bounce while it chewed. The time was seventeen minutes past one and thirty-four seconds.

Zabdiel Seinfeld was signing off a phone call with a member of the executive board of directors at two minutes past two. They'd discussed the newly hired PR staff. The hiring decisions had been made and they were in the process of contacting the relevant people. There was some discussion about the relevancy of the new staff under the threat of an oncoming Yellow Orang-Utan Industries financial crisis. The board had assured Zabdiel Seinfeld that they were keenly aware of the breaking issues, relevant board members had convened and discussed the issue within minutes of the company lawyers controversially meeting with the shareholder's lawyers, and structured recruitment tactics catering to Zabdiel Seinfeld's Yellow Orang-Utan.

The president of Yellow Orang-Utan Industries listened in on the whole thing. He was still listening when Zabdiel signed off at two past two. He thought for a moment then typed instructions into his computer program so Zabdiel Seinfeld would place another call. He called a senior member of the PR department. He claimed that firstly he was calling to assure that the replacement staff would soon join the department and their recruitment was being based on their experiences with similar situations to the one Yellow Orang-Utan was facing. The PR official assured Zabdiel Seinfeld he was well aware of this decision, having been consulted and briefed by the board of directors. Assurances aside, the PR employee warned that no experience could equal working for the biggest corporation in the world, Yellow Orang-Utan Industries was legendary. Zabdiel graciously accepted the flattery on behalf of their organisation and moved on to inquire about the Dinosaurs 'R' Us news story.

Gertrude listened along with the president. Was the news story a PR exercise, did it come from their department? Apparently not, the story was as new to the PR department as it was the rest of Yellow Orang-Utan. The Telly-net reports were genuine articles and not mock ups from the corporation. Zabdiel Seinfeld cordially signed off from the phone call. The president leant back in his chair.

"I must admit Gertrude," called the president, "I did take your friends' advice from the other day and things seem to be going well. Thanks for the tip." Gertrude smiled.

"Thank you sir." She rubbed her leg. The time was ten minutes past two and twelve seconds.

At quarter to seven that evening Biscuit received a knock on her door. She smiled, leapt up from her couch and answered the door. Through its frame she could see Wellington, smiling back at her and with arms wrapped around take away food. She had him enter her apartment without much coaxing. They spread the food out on her coffee table. They watched the Telly-net monitor that had been on since Biscuit had arrived there after her day at work. Biscuit was distracted by the entertainment on display so that it was a while before she began to eat the food. She laughed many times on her way to eventually lifting her chopsticks. In an effort to be a polite host and to impress Wellington, she pried her attention away from the monitor enough to engage the robot in a little conversation.

"Why do you bother eating? I know you're a robot," she inquired. Wellington had only begun eating when Biscuit had, the food had cooled to lukewarm temperatures by then but was very spicy.

"It's just social protocol programming. The way people drink socially when they're not thirsty," Wellington answered. Biscuit slowly fed herself mouthfuls of the spicy food and watched the robot she had a crush on do the same.

"Did you see much of the Yellow Orang-Utan Industries news today?" Asked Wellington, aware of a growing silence between mouthfuls and the discomfort flesh and blood humans can have with lengthy pauses in social situations.

"It wasn't very good, was it?" Biscuit remarked.

"It wasn't all bad," suggested Wellington. "The reports are very dramatic, but it isn't exactly as catastrophic as they're making it out to be."

"Oh?" replied Biscuit, half expecting a gabfest from Wellington.

"Well, we are going to lose our biggest investor, and with them gone, the others will probably follow suit. But this won't mean Yellow Orang-Utan Industries will completely collapse. It would take a lot more to reduce the world's biggest corporation to nothing. What's being dramatised on the news is perhaps the possibility that Yellow Orang-Utan Industries isn't going to be the world's largest corporation anymore. Considering how long that's been the case, it is an event of sorts, should it happen. It'll upset the scheme of things, economically speaking." Wellington paused politely, it sort of compensated for not needing to breathe while he talked. His facial expression adjusted to accept interjection from Biscuit. She finished a mouthful of spicy noodles.

"That's not all, is it?" Suggested Biscuit, half playfully. Wellington grinned, interpreting Biscuit's understanding.

"Remember that night in the place where we had coffee?" asked Wellington.

"Yes, what was that place called? I don't remember," stated Biscuit.

"Neither do I," Wellington replied.

"But surely a robot such as yourself would remember?" Suggested Biscuit.

"Pepi and I randomly erase small details like that, otherwise my portable memory drive fills up as I absorb information all day." The robot explained. "What I do remember is significant information about

Dinosaurs 'R' Us that I'd told you that night."

"I remember that, I told Gertrude. But what was that about? You were talking crazy talk that night." Biscuit looked into her take away carton at the greasy meat and vegetables surrounded by noodles.

"I said it needs to be sold off, we have to cease our connection with it. Today on the news programs the sale was reported increasingly. It was quite a positive report." Wellington reached for Biscuit's Telly-net monitor remote control. He searched amongst the menu and found the news sites. Skimming through them he found a report on the sale. It went on to profile the board of executive directors at Yellow Orang-Utan Industries in a pleasant manner, rather than the scathing nature of reports on Zabdiel Seinfeld.

"This is just what I predicted would happen," he said, looking earnestly at Biscuit. Biscuit took the remote control from her friend and turned off the monitor.

"Eat your dinner," she commanded cheekily. He did and so did she.

"I've figured out what needs to happen next," Wellington announced when the empty cartons were returned to the coffee table.

"What?" asked Biscuit.

"When Zabdiel Seinfeld goes on Telly-net again, he needs to mention orange juice."

"Is that it?" Biscuit asked.

"Yes, it's as simple as selling off Dinosaurs 'R' Us was and it should be as effective," assured the robot sincerely. Biscuit sighed.

"Thanks Wellington, thanks very much. Are you coming to Fishpaste tonight?" Biscuit got up from the couch to look down at him.

"I'm not going out there anymore. I'm going back to the Yellow Orang-Utan building after this," replied Wellington. Biscuit pouted, then whined.

"We've discussed this with Pepi, it's too risky. Someone else might find out I'm a robot, I did hurt your feelings when you found out," the robot reminded the secretary.

"But I don't mind now, neither does Gertrude," Biscuit whinged.

"Even so, Pepi could get in lots of trouble if people from Yellow Orang-Utan find out I'm working there fraudulently," warned Wellington. He stood up.

"Help me pick out what I'm going to wear before you go," instructed Biscuit. She disappeared around a doorway. Wellington stood alone in the lounge room and waited. Minutes later he pointed and said: "That one." She'd held up two evening gowns on hangers, she dropped one to the floor. Biscuit removed what remained of her current outfit and slipped into the drapery of the still aloft hanger. She had meant to tease Wellington, not that he could be, but at a quarter to nine – Wellington the robot politely shifted his gaze away from the changing woman.

Prudence was kissing her new boyfriend at twelve minutes past nine and ten seconds. She was in good company with her friends Gertrude and Sensae nearby. Sensae had his usual hangers on and Gertrude had attracted a small crowd of adoring gentlemen to join their party. Eventually she stopped kissing her boyfriend. Biscuit entered the nightclub and Prudence waved at her. Then Gertrude and Sensae waved at her and she got closer to them and greeted them with polite kisses.

"I think Prudence is going to have an early night," Gertrude said to Biscuit while Prudence returned her gaze into her new love. "You'll have to help me dance with these guys soon. They want to dance, they've been pestering me." Biscuit looked around the booth at her assembled company, she leaned over to Sensae.

"Whatever you guys are on, I want in," she demanded. Sensae grinned.

"Sorry, I'm fresh out," he apologised. Biscuit scowled.

"Buy me a tequila then," bargained the young woman. Sensae excused himself from his seat and escorted Biscuit to the bar. Gertrude laughed at something one of her suitors said. Prudence identified her drink from amongst the others on a table and sipped at it with renewed attention. Sensae and Biscuit knocked back their drinks at the bar and returned to their familiar party.

Gertrude and Biscuit led the young men to the dance floor, Gertrude making hasty introductions along the way. They began dancing. Sensae remarked to his hangers on and Prudence's boyfriend that they probably wouldn't see them back here for a while, now that they were dancing. Prudence joined the dancers then her boyfriend joined Prudence. Sensae sighed and watched them play. They began to dance cheekily, then as the music changed, sexily. Sensae, bored watching, reluctantly joined them too. He'd noticed the young men dancing with Gertrude and Biscuit had been growing restless, although some were dancing very close to Gertrude and they seemed to be enjoying that, as had Gertrude. But not long after Sensae had joined the dancing party, one of them tapped a wristwatch and started bothering others about leaving. When they eventually exited *Fishpaste*, some were very apologetic. But the remains of the party, the regulars, returned to their booth and caught their breath.

So Prudence started kissing her boyfriend again. Biscuit convinced Sensae to buy her another drink. Something more thirst quenching after the dancing than tequila. Gertrude began to joke and gossip with Sensae's hangers on who'd sat through all the dancing like obedient pets. But then Sensae and Biscuit returned to the booth and table with their drinks and Gertrude started chatting with them. But then between chatter, as Biscuit and Sensae sipped their drinks, Gertrude got thirsty and went to get a drink too. When all their drinks were at the table and finished or close to it, Gertrude and Biscuit hit the dance floor again. Finally, Prudence and her boyfriend left for more private quarters.

Ted Showbiz, the ever-present *Fishpaste* dance floor occupant, moved closer to the two dancers called Biscuit and Gertrude. Biscuit looked to Gertrude for some judgement. Gertrude nodded approval. The two pretty women let the fat drunk dance with them. Gertrude who had visited this place as nearly as often as Ted did, had never actually danced with this guy. The staff from the club were surprised to see it. Ted hadn't become any better behaved, but Gertrude had changed, perhaps, a little. But as soon as his hands got too friendly with Biscuit, they quickly dashed back to the booth, giggling. Ted stood still on the glowing floor of Telly-net shows and waved the familiar nightclub princesses goodbye at eleven O' five.

At twenty-five minutes past one Biscuit and Gertrude sat in the back of a moving taxi.

"You could lose your job," Gertrude exclaimed.

"It's not that bad, Wellington said," replied Biscuit. Gertrude gasped.

"You saw Wellington?"

"Yes! He came over for dinner, with me. I showed him my boobs." Biscuit replied.

"No!" exclaimed a tired and inebriated personal assistant to the president of Yellow Orang-Utan Industries.

"Yes, I did. I showed him my boobs. I made him pick this dress and I put it on in front of him. He said the stuff on the news about work isn't as bad as it appears," continued Biscuit.

"He's a robot."

"I know."

"Biscoe," began Gertrude.

"Yes?" egged Biscuit in a funny voice.

"I work with the president so I think I know that there is gonna be some people who are going to lose their jobs. I've got inside information." Gertrude winked at Biscuit and tapped the side of her nose.

"Wellington's pretty clever though," Biscuit remarked.

"I know," the taxi stopped. It was by Biscuit's apartment building. She figured that out then paid the taxi driver, pecked Gertrude on the cheek goodbye then rummaged through her handbag for her keys. Gertrude spoke to all assembled in the taxi within earshot where to take her next, it careered off at twenty-nine minutes past one and fifty-five seconds.

18.

At the broadest level, this leads to the central concern being the so-called 'problem of social order', for an organism is clearly not a real organisation at all (or at any rate not a healthy one) if its component parts fight with one another, fail to operate, or drop off.

At nine twenty-one in the morning, Gertrude stood quietly by a comfy chair in a hallway large enough to be considered a foyer. There was a table next to the comfy chair with a fake plant in a real pot on it. Behind her were some closed doors and behind the closed doors sat the president of Yellow Orang-Utan Industries, and the vice presidents of Yellow Orang-Utan Industries and members of the board of executive directors of Yellow Orang-Utan Industries. Gertrude was none of those things. She was a personal assistant. As were Palmira and Madison, who were also standing in the hallway. Oakley had ensured Palmira's continued employment with a new member of the Yellow Orang-Utan board, as she had wished. She looked bored while Gertrude looked thoughtful and Madison looked stern, as she quietly maintained businesslike conversation on a phone. Other PAs or secretaries were about, all barred from their immediate superiors by the closed doors, others had returned to their offices to relay important information via workstations.

Inside, the most senior staff of the company, who arranged the bigger shifts and trends that would ramify throughout departments ensconced in the big building and many other offices throughout the world, were choosing their words very carefully. The president sat by Naamah in complete silence as a video screen with the image of Zabdiel Seinfeld did the talking for him. They were trying to address the issues concerning major ventures, reconfigured by the dwindling support. Zabdiel Seinfeld, of course, steered the conversation with aplomb.

The brains and mouths of upper management whirred away for some time. Outside in the big hallway, some assistants had abandoned their posts by the closed doors and returned to their workstations, their numbers dwindling like outside support for the company. Gertrude now sat down in the comfy chair by the table with the fake plant in the real pot. Eventually the important company figureheads emerged as the closed doors became open. They were still commenting and laughing as Zabdiel Seinfeld, and a few others, had made some final remarks that had offered a positive closing statement that bonded them as people with a shared aim and vision. They made eye contact with their respective staff who had remained in the hallway. The president looked at Gertrude. She stood up from the comfy chair.

"Geez, I need a coffee," he said at ten fifty-three.

At ten past one Biscuit and Gertrude stood in line at a noodle bar not far from the Yellow Orang-Utan building. Biscuit knew especially that it was ten past one as she was checking her time piece, attempting to predict the average waiting time of the line. They discussed the menu of the venue before Gertrude changed the subject.

"I think it's getting worse upstairs, Biscoe," she confessed, "there was a fairly heavy meeting today." Biscuit was still staring intently at the menu.

"Hmm?" she replied.

"I think it's getting worse, I feel like it's going to end. I'm really considering seriously I might not be working for Yellow Orang-Utan in the future," Gertrude repeated.

"Well, I think you're being a bit serious about it," replied Biscuit, still distracted by the lunch menu.

"Maybe you're being too flippant," returned Gertrude, a little dissatisfied she wasn't getting Biscuit's full attention, but not to the point of anger. Biscuit turned to her and smiled.

"Even, if, you were to lose a Yellow Orang-Utan job. Don't you think that dorky little guy you work for would hire you out of his own pocket? He'd be lost without you, hmm?" she replied, Gertrude smiled back and conceded. Biscuit got distracted again as they got their food served. They found a small clean table in the noodle bar and sat together over their contained noodles.

"There was a fairly heavy meeting this morning, I wasn't allowed in, I just had to sit outside and wait with the other PAs. I think they're preparing some kind of exit strategy," Gertrude resumed.

"Exit out of what?" asked Biscuit.

"Well, the marketplace. I think they're planning to sell off their excised subsidiaries and then gear up to sell off whatever's left over as the core of the business," replied Gertrude blankly. Biscuit looked back at Gertrude wide eyed and in shock.

"You know," Biscuit began, "if you and I hadn't spent so much time with Wellington these past few months, I wouldn't have had a clue what you're talking about. Did you just hear yourself?" Gertrude giggled, Biscuit inhaled.

"OK firstly, Yellow Orang-Utan is too big for anyone to just buy. They're the biggest. No one else is big enough to just buy what they're worth. When Yellow Orang-Utan has a bad day on the market, it's pretty much guaranteed the rest of the market is having a terrible day. Which is why I'm not nearly as frightful as you are about my job. Secondly, having had such quality time with our robot friend I would argue, whatever trouble Yellow Orang-Utan gets itself into, I'm pretty sure Wellington can get it out again. He is a genius robot." Biscuit reached for the juice she'd bought with her lunch. Gertrude smiled.

"Well", said Gertrude, "I'm pretty sure that bad day on the market stuff hasn't been the same since Piano Smedley passed on. We've been going down under Zabdiel Seinfeld while other big companies are on the rise. If

Yellow Orang-Utan does begin selling off its assets, it may become small enough for something big to acquire it. It'll take a while, but it could reach that point, we might not see within our own time at Yellow Orang-Utan but, I mean, nothing lasts forever. On the Wellington side of things though, I agree with you completely." Biscuit nodded in agreement.

"And I'm very impressed with what geniuses we are for having such a grown up discussion," Gertrude added.

"We're stock market experts," agreed Biscuit. The pair high-fived each other, surrounding diners suddenly felt a lack of exuberant camaraderie in their choice of lunch companion.

A few hearty mouthfuls later they resumed their talk.

"Wellington probably doesn't have the security clearance to make as big a difference as you're imagining though, Biscoe," suggested Gertrude.

"I suppose, but the stuff he does is so subtle and small and random, he's already made big waves that one time? Remember?" Biscuit said, licking her lips and feeling self conscious, when Gertrude licked her lips it looked sexy and cool.

"Of course I remember, I told my boss about it before anything got done. Wellington couldn't quite do it, but now that it has been done, it's been pretty good. There's supposed to be this big deal profile on the new board of directors on the Telly-net tonight," Gertrude added.

"Are you going to watch it?" asked Biscuit. Gertrude thought about it.

"Probably not," was her calculated response. They ate some more.

"Wellington said that Zabdiel Seinfeld needs to mention orange juice in his next media appearance." Biscuit announced as she neared the end of the meal, her chopstick dexterity was climaxing.

"You mean for all that market stuff? To increase Yellow Orang-Utan's market value, Zabdiel Seinfeld needs to be associated with orange juice?" asked Gertrude.

"Something like that," confirmed Biscuit. Gertrude wiped her mouth.

"Well, I'll be sure to pass that on," she said slyly. Their lunch was soon finished and they rose from their small dining table to return to the Yellow Orang-Utan Industries building at forty-two minutes past one in the afternoon.

At twenty minutes past four the president of Yellow Orang-Utan Industries was reflecting on the day. There'd been meetings and memos and a lot of it working the software he needed to operate Zabdiel Seinfeld in a professional manner. A great deal of time had been spent in front of this software interface, now that things were back to normal. Yet, what he'd been using Zabdiel Seinfeld for lately wasn't something he'd ever done with Piano Smedley. This morning he'd begun to orchestrate the downscaling of the biggest company in the world. They were selling off non-core assets. The new board of executive directors were now hatching plans with the global resources of Yellow Orang-Utan and their own networks gleaned from experienced careers, to negotiate the strip down of Yellow Orang-Utan. The president wasn't entirely sure if this was going back to normal.

Gertrude sat on the far side of the room, patiently watching and waiting for a task from her superior, the president. The president could see Gertrude if he peered past a screen on his workstation.

"Is anything the matter, Gertrude?" he had to ask, he was sure there was something she wanted to say. Gertrude sighed, realigned her posture and looked at the president of Yellow Orang-Utan Industries. Then she looked at him, slyly, in a way the president wasn't used to seeing in Gertrude.

"My friend gave me another investment tip," was the sound that emanated from the suspiciously composed Gertrude. The president of Yellow Orang-Utan smiled to himself, pretended to be engrossed in his work screen a little longer before returning her knowing look.

"What have you heard this time?" asked the old businessman.

"Erm, this one's a little strange," she replied. The president smiled again.

"What is it?"

"Hmm, I've heard, that...Zabdiel should mention orange juice on Telly-net." Gertrude felt her composure shrink, "I'm not sure I understand it myself."

"That is strange. Normally an investment tip involves investing in something, buying or selling, something along those lines. Where did you hear such things?"

"I'm not even sure now, it might not have been the same person," Gertrude stammered, she staved off her humiliation knowing in some ways she was protecting Wellington.

"Well, I suppose that wouldn't hurt, mentioning orange juice, would it?" offered the president. They both laughed quietly. She reminded herself this advice was in the interest of Yellow Orang-Utan and in that way, in her employment interests, at four fifty-nine.

The president had dismissed Gertrude at three minutes past five and was still clicking around his workstation screen at five thirty-seven and two seconds. Soon his dinner delivery would arrive, he'd perhaps laser himself clean and change himself before settling down to another evening in front of the Wall-span TV. There'd be journalists reacting to his company all night long, which was kind of his idea of fun. Meanwhile, he was still clicking around for Zabdiel to do this and that amongst the departments ensconced in his building, with a few other buildings around the world to communicate with too. The president felt righteous, and a tad hungry, and he needed to pee, but he thought as an act of goodwill, before he followed up his physical cravings, he programmed orange juice into Zabdiel's keywords for his next Telly-net appearance. The president of Yellow Orang-Utan Industries shut down his computer and left his desk for another room. At six in the evening, he urinated.

The president had assumed his relaxed frown by three minutes to eight later that evening. He'd slumped into a comfy recess of his bed while the Telly-net droned on. The dinner he'd had warmed his belly, the nourishment coursing through his brains providing contentment. The journalists were shaking their heads when their show's content steered toward talking about Zabdiel Seinfeld and Yellow Orang-Utan. It made him think of his flaccid penis, which didn't concern him nearly as much now. Now he felt old and wise, and would mentally dismiss the stern voices of the popular financial analysts before him. He felt like an old monk, and monks often seemed very content and happy, and they were often celibate, erections didn't matter.

In any case there were occasional good news stories about Yellow Orang-Utan, like the positive profiling of the new board of executive directors that had been on. Thinking back though, the president realised that had been linked to the episode concerning the sale of Dinosaurs 'R' Us. Then he remembered entering orange juice into a selection of keywords for Zabdiel Seinfeld's next Telly-net appearance. When that would occur exactly in his news feed he wasn't quite sure, but now he was waiting for it to happen. Satisfied as he was with his resolve that Zabdiel Seinfeld had an authentic, original new direction, he felt the orange juice move was something more akin to Zabdiel's predecessor. Allowable because it seemed irrelevant, but all the more perverse a pleasure. Then it happened, Zabdiel Seinfeld appeared unto the president of Yellow Orang-Utan Industries on the Wall-span television and mentioned orange juice. The president chuckled. It was at eight forty-three that evening, that was the time.

At about five minutes past nine, storeys below the president of Yellow Orang-Utan Industries, Pepito sat in a small office with Wellington watching Telly-net. Someone else on their monitor was mentioning orange juice, a reaction to a sound byte elicited by Zabdiel Seinfeld. Pepito was a little lost for words, everything Wellington claimed could happen was playing out before his eyes on the monitor. The robot he'd put together was deciphering messages from information sources in ways he didn't begin to understand. Furthermore, the robot was watching the report with an intensity uncommon with the robots he'd researched before building the robot.

"Wellington," Pepito began.

"Yes?" the robot politely replied.

"You don't need to watch the Telly-net so seriously. Ah, I mean, your face. You don't need to display such emotion around me." Wellington looked up at Pepito briefly and adjusted his demeanour.

"Sorry, Pepi, the news is about Yellow Orang-Utan. It's where I work, I thought it would be normal to feign interest."

"And the orange juice thing was your idea too?" Pepito continued. "Yes."

"I suppose you'd have a right to wear such a face." Pepito looked again at his robot that was again concentrating on the Telly-net monitor in

Pepito's modest office.

"It's all going to plan, I suppose?" asked Pepito.

"It's just as I had predicted." Wellington replied flatly.

"I've heard orange juice a lot," remarked Pepito.

"That's OK, that's how it would happen," Pepito's robot assured him. They heard orange juice mentioned again. Pepito smiled a little.

"You're too good at this, Wellington." Pepito questioned himself often as to why he'd hid Wellington in the market hacker department, rather than somewhere else in the corporation. While he was ensuring everybody had the machines and the programs running to make Yellow Orang-Utan work, the market hackers got to move the investments around to make the corporation bigger and bigger and make the news every evening. Often those news reports consisted of content provided by the programs that came from his department. He'd been part of or led groups that developed the means to seamlessly insert Yellow Orang-Utan spin, embodied now as Zabdiel Seinfeld, into news reports and communication all around the building he sat in now and around the world. But the discussion in the media usually laid their laurels on the heroes of the market. Wellington was a superbly anonymous market hacker. Pepito had set out to build a better hero. He liked to imagine the potential of Wellington's agency as if Wellington was the face in the Telly-net rather than Zabdiel Seinfeld, but tonight Wellington had managed to put words in Seinfeld's mouth without any assistance from Pepito which, although still proud, slightly frightened him.

"Pepi," Wellington said, interrupting Pepito's thoughts, Pepito raised his eyebrows waiting for Wellington.

"If I had the access, I could capitalise on this and probably generate a lot of investment in Yellow Orang-Utan. Enough to compensate for the large losses the company's had in recent weeks."

"Enough access? Enough to remain low profile?"

"I could rearrange my investment strategies in order to eventually gain the scale of interest I'm talking about from my current access level. It would take longer, but I could do it given time. However, it would not be low profile for someone of my access level to single-handedly usher in what could be described as a pretty dramatic windfall, and I'm not sure I have the time." Wellington was clever, Pepito was suspicious and couldn't help but feel conservative.

"You've worked around your access issues, Wellington, everybody on that monitor's been mentioning orange juice, haven't they?" Pepito cautioned.

"Zabdiel Seinfeld's business trends, without any further influence, could lose more investment than the company's already recently had. It does seem like the direction he's trying to author is that of downsizing a lot of our operations and subsidiaries. You programmed me to work as a market hacker at Yellow Orang-Utan. I can't do that if my position is made redundant, or relevant colleagues such as yourself, or entire departments. People will lose jobs. How soon that happens will be relative to how well we keep what ventures we still have afloat, or any possible new ventures. A lot of ventures depend on varying levels of access, access I don't necessarily have. I can work to maintain what we have with the access I currently hold, but my success rate is relative to limitations of time, my security access levels and the professional profile I'm trying to maintain within Yellow Orang-Utan." Wellington waved his hand at the monitor, where an opinionated journalist was seconding Wellington's theories about Zabdiel Seinfeld, and the decreasing power of Yellow Orang-Utan Industries.

"And if I just gave you log in codes for your market hacker programs that would let you operate as someone with higher access? Would you use them?" Pepito had already wiped portions of Wellington's memory to allow space for another day's information and prevent Wellington from coming across as an infallible, artificial genius with a perfect photographic memory. Despite these measures, too many evenings ended with Wellington drawing the same conclusion.

"It may not be ethical," the robot offered. Wellington then produced from a pocket the small black card he'd negotiated as part of his market hacker contract many months ago and placed it on the same table where the monitor was positioned.

"But," Wellington added, "dramatic windfall." The time was nine thirty-seven.

19.

What remains is the threat of unmet deadlines, social rejection and anxiety about missing the last train home.

By eleven O' clock and eight minutes the president was in his room, on the end of his luxurious bed watching the news on his Wall-span TV. Gertrude, meanwhile, was ordering their lunch. There was more news afoot concerning Yellow Orang-Utan. The orange juice sound-byte was working, Wellington had made crucial transactions that were manageable with standard security access levels on market hacker software on a descendant floor. The news was on the Telly-net, a little man watching the news on a big bed was a little surprised, his mouth opened a little. He had to get up and use his desk to contact relevant departments and personnel to confirm the stories, organise briefing reports to be sent to Zabdiel Seinfeld's e-mail address. As the news barrelled on, the Yellow Orang-Utan president scurried back to the bed to watch the giant Wall-span screen as news feeds repeated themselves again and again. So absorbed in the news gilded with his secret conceit that Gertrude had to similarly repeat herself over and over to compete.

"Lunch has arrived," Gertrude said, again, with a raised voice. The president turned his head.

"Already?" he asked.

"It's twelve-thirty," she pointed out. They each glanced at respective time pieces, he'd lost track of time.

"Crocodile pie?"

"With cheese and chilli sauce." Gertrude turned to head to their usual dining facility.

"Be right there," the president said while watching Gertrude's bottom make its way to the boardroom. They each reached their meals and then tucked in. Halfway through his pie the president sat back, savouring the meat. He looked across the table at his assistant. He chewed.

"Gertrude," she glanced up at him, tucking into a forkful of fish and salad.

"Thank you for the tip the other day, about the orange juice. I know I put it down at the time. But, and I can't explain it, I executed it anyway. I didn't think it would really make any difference one way or another. But there's been some very good news today, you can probably tell, I'm pretty distracted with it today. And I can't explain, that is, I'm not sure, I'm trying to get confirmation or a link or something." He sighed.

"I'm suspicious the good news, somehow, had to do with whatever it was you told me and whatever it was I did with that information. I have no idea otherwise why this has happened. So Gertrude, it would help me, a lot, if you could tell me where you got the idea." Gertrude swallowed a mouthful of lunch and cast a speculative look at her employer.

"Um, I can ask around, I guess. I mean, it came second hand to me, you know?"

"Yes," the president answered, "I suppose it starts like a rumour, spreads the same too. But I think it's going to be really important that we can get a handle on the source. I guess that's an order Gertrude, please, ask around."

"OK," she said.

"And thank you for telling me in the first place, once again, thanks." They resumed eating and the time was twelve forty-seven.

By six O' nine, Pepito had completed his required tasks for his day job at Yellow Orang-Utan Industries. Pepito was considering changing Wellington's security clearance. He had not been looking forward to it. It had been distracting, and leading up to the end of the day, stressful. He had created an agent of artificial intelligence, equipped via programming of independent thought, and he was trying to patch together in his mind how that intelligence was thinking and acting. He wanted to get his head around Wellington, if that was possible, without having to build more robots. The programming by which Wellington walked, talked and mirrored social customs, Pepito understood, how Wellington consumed and interpreted information, Pepito understood, how he'd structured memory banks and processors to contain and co-ordinate this information, Pepito understood. But how this collection of co-operating programs combined to apparently make a robot that could predict the stock market in unheard of ways he couldn't quite grasp.

Computer analysis was already widespread and common across all manner of business long before Yellow Orang-Utan began, with obvious influences on the decisions businesses made. There was a chance companies all around the world were developing programs to achieve what Wellington appeared to do. As far as Pepito had read though, there hadn't been any public precedents. That would be a simple resolution to what Pepito was worried about. If he could translate Wellington's programming into something he could run across a computer, Wellington wouldn't need suspicious extra security clearances. Pepito could install something like Wellington's analytic engines in the Zabdiel Seinfeld program, and it could operate with the autonomy allowed by the president, normal for that program. Except the external influences that Wellington encountered, that were organised along with all the Telly-net feeds, weren't as easily reproduced as news media. Wellington still walked around and had real time conversations with people, whereas a program would be stuck in one spot. Could the real world comings and goings be substituted? Perhaps Wellington could feed the program that information?

The ideas in his head would take time to develop, and Wellington had stressed they perhaps didn't have time. Pepito stopped thinking, leaned back in his chair and engulfed a lot of temperature conditioned oxygen. The discovery of Wellington might cost Pepito's job, but if Wellington was right, Pepito might lose his job anyway. Then, Wellington could also be completely wrong, Yellow Orang-Utan could still be doomed and perhaps nobody would find out anything. It didn't really matter. Pepito laughed and made a phone call. The synthesized voice of Wellington was heard when the call was answered.

"Hallo? Wellington speaking," was the answer.

"Hi Wellington, it's Pepi," Pepito began.

"Hallo Pepi." Pepito wondered if Wellington would detect some kind of craziness in his voice, he suspected he was feeling glimmers of euphoria.

"I'm ready to give you the security clearance you need to help us all at Yellow Orang-Utan industries."

"Really? That is good news."

"Yeah, there's a few options we can discuss. Are you finished for the day?"

"Nearly."

"Well get up here so I can empty out your memory and tummy-bag, yeah?"

"OK, I'll be there soon after your security door opens at exactly six twenty."

The time was six O' clock and sixteen minutes.

At six forty-four the president of Yellow Orang-Utan was tucking into his dinner, delivered to his quarters quickly after being prepared professionally from the healthiest of ingredients. Small packages of food

134

were scattered around a table that once hosted some of history's more prestigious business meetings, the president wiped his lips. The packages were nearly empty, sauces smeared their insides. The president's mind had not been on his food, which he gobbled without savour, because thankfully he was still thinking about an important report he'd been reading that afternoon.

There had been a section at the back of the report that the president had deliberately not read. As darkness fell and his belly bulged, he began the slide toward the indulgences of creature comforts, it was time to read that bit. He finished what remained desirable of his dinner, laser-cleaned himself in the bathroom, managed to locate and dress into comfortable evening wear and crawled across his big bed to pick up the book-sized report there. He read and perceived the work clearly, it was mostly about the sale of Dinosaurs 'R' Us, it was interesting. The analysis was thorough, the attractive charts illustrated concepts throughout. However, as he read, a furrow in his brow appeared and grew firmer. This section compared the business activity with Zabdiel Seinfeld's leadership and direction, keeping in tone with the rest of the report. But the charts introduced remarkably different patterns and as it continued the tone of the rest of the report, there was insinuation growing in the language. The bulk of the prior report had continually referred to this. It had the president reassessing the prior material. Pages flipped faster, his nostrils flared as much as his old skin allowed. The president exhaled noisily and put the report down. That felt better, he reached around and found the controller for the Wall-span TV, to fill his head with something a little more relaxing than the report.

Professionally photographed news-anchors and digitally animated avatars alike spiralled towards him bearing headlines and sound bytes. The seemingly positive message they bore was of some large impending investment in Yellow Orang-Utan industries. The specific link seemed tenuous, but as each channel, each feed, told the story with varying degrees of context, somebody mentioned orange juice, paraphrasing or directly from Zabdiel Seinfeld footage. The president knew he'd authored it, with no idea of the ramifications he witnessed now on the Wall-span TV. Now, he felt sick.

He thought of Gertrude to make himself feel better, and he could think up affirming platitudes all night, but what was playing out before him on the gargantuan screen generated enough doubt to undo them all. He turned off the TV. He stared at the report and, with a sigh, picked it up again. The president scanned the document further, seeking answers to the non-specific questions clouding his head. He finished the section at the back. Even with a natural nocturnal drive for sleep gaining momentum, he went back and read earlier parts he'd skipped and some he'd already read with a renewed scrutiny. By the time he put the finished report down, the president's mind was delirious, he couldn't stop thinking. He didn't know what time he actually fell asleep, but it was twenty-three minutes past two.

At ten twenty-one earlier that evening, Pepito's phone rang in his pocket and he began fishing it out. Kilometres away, Gertrude had been pressing buttons on the connecting phone.

"Hello?" Pepito managed through a mouthful of reheated food.

"Pepi? Hi, it's Gertrude," was the response to management.

"I know, Hi," Pepito replied, swallowing. There was a tiny pause.

"Um, today at work my boss, uh, he asked about Wellington," Gertrude began, "I mean, the investing stuff. He's been talking to Biscoe about it, she mentions it to me and, uh, I mention it to my boss." The sound of Pepito's breath translated itself down the line, Gertrude listened carefully, worried about his reaction. Then he said "OK", and she felt tiny relief. He said "OK" again, and then laughed.

"I've already talked to Wellington tonight. In fact, I'm giving him free reign now, he's got all the access he wants. Should I go see a lawyer? I'm already going to go see a lawyer. First thing tomorrow, probably." Pepito chortled. Gertrude responded with a pause, Pepito half-noticed.

"So, what I think I'm getting at Gertrude, is, uh, I'll need to call a meeting. I need to tell your boss, or Zabdiel or whatever and tell the right people about Wellington."

"Right. A meeting, I can do that. That, I guess, makes things easier for me." She expected this to be harder, she had felt uncomfortable with the implications of exposing Pepito and Wellington's secret, but her and Pepi's timing seemed perfect.

"I guess, you and me and your boss, or Zabdiel, and Wellington. I can brief and debrief and spill my guts about Wellington and what he's achieved so far. I can be completely honest now, secrets seem a bit silly at the moment, what with the directions the company seems to be heading in. Wellington is potentially a lot of good news, he's certainly helped create a lot already with very little clearance." Gertrude listened to Pepito's voice through the connection, she could hear it wavering slightly, perhaps there was still something to be uncomfortable about.

"Well, I can get my boss there tomorrow, probably Zabdiel too if you think that's necessary, that should be easy," she responded. There was a pause, Pepito had stopped talking enough to hear what Gertrude just said and then, amidst processes already rushing his mind since earlier that evening, understood what she said and what that would mean.

"Thank you, Gertrude. Thanks a lot," he said.

"No problem, Pepi. I'll arrange a time and message you first thing tomorrow." Gertrude was perhaps relaxing, she smiled.

"Alright, Gertrude. See you tomorrow." Pepito pressed buttons on his phone and returned it to his pocket. Yes, he would talk to a lawyer tomorrow and confess everything to his employer. But the rest of the evening would be dedicated to not caring anymore, and this was so liberating, so exhilarating, he wondered if he'd achieve a single wink of sleep. The time was currently ten thirty in the night and it would be eleven before Pepito would even see a clock.

At eleven thirty-eight in the night, somewhere inside the Yellow Orang-Utan Industries information technology laboratory, a screen illuminated the operator of a computer. The operator was another computer, there was a power cable attached to this other computer that, via a socket in a wall and via an industrial size electrical turbine many kilometres away, was powering its computations as well as charging an internal battery. The battery helped operate the computer independently of power cables, as during the day the computer would often move freely about the rest of the Yellow Orang-Utan Industries building. This didn't seem unusual to the many employees of Yellow Orang-Utan Industries who also moved freely about the building during the day, as most of them were similarly capable of automatic robotic movement. Furthermore, most of the time, with very few exceptions, the computer maintained the outward appearance of the other employees. Its outward casing adopted humanoid design, wore complimenting clothing with popular scents, as well as the latest in synthetic hair and skins recommended by plastic surgeons. If addressed by a fellow employee, it could automatically converse with highly adapted animatronic tools and appropriate mimicking and psych-reading software. Although at this time of night, free from the presence of other employees, this was less relevant to the computer's current task. It was operating its mimicking and psych-reading software, cross checking information it was entering into the other computer. The illumination from the screen of the other computer, revealed the identity of its operating computer, it was Wellington. On the screen was an avatar that represented, to the general public as well as every employee at Yellow Orang-Utan, or more specifically within the software program's interface for the president of Yellow Orang-Utan, Zabdiel Seinfeld. Less relevant to charging Wellington, but also on the nameless computer's screen, in one corner, the time counted out the minutes Wellington spent programming the Zabdiel Seinfeld software. At one point that time was one fifteen in the AM.

20.

To secure investment it is vital that you understand their role, read their guidelines and form a relationship with the relevant investment manager.

Gertrude had awoken the president of Yellow Orang-Utan Industries at ten past nine in the morning. She had seen to it that the president had washed and dressed. Upon his request, Gertrude then fetched him a coffee and ordered him some breakfast. She'd grabbed herself a batch of fruits, nuts and cereals amalgamated by a mysterious synthetic sticky stuff, and a few pills, before leaving her apartment earlier that morning. The president's breakfast had arrived and he took the breakfast while Gertrude sometimes watched him eat, sometimes discussed a scheduled meeting for that morning and sometimes looked at her clipboard where she'd listed a meeting for the president with Pepito, and Wellington. The president, after breakfast, read emails between distracting segue-ways of Telly-net news stories. By then it was almost ten O' clock in the morning. At that time, the president's telephone rang.

"Hello?" The president hailed into its mouthpiece.

"Naamah here," was the corresponding hail.

"Hi Naamah, how are you this morning? Did you get any breakfast?" The president's lips were still greasy from this morning's foodstuffs.

"Good morning sir, breakfast was, uh, fine. Erm, have you been in the Zabdiel Seinfeld program today?" The president of Yellow Orang-Utan had to think about it.

"Er, no. I don't believe so," he slowly replied, and then in response to the seriousness of Naamah's detectable tone asked "is there something wrong?" Gertrude watched as the president fumbled with his hardware trying to open a particular program.

"It just seems that Zabdiel has an unusually full schedule. I've checked with Letitia and neither of us have entered anything beyond our normal activities," continued the vice president, "and I was debriefing with Seinfeld before I left yesterday and there wasn't much on the cards. So unless you've entered some new directives overnight, I'm, I'm a bit confused where this schedule came from. I mean the security access level of this program is very high. Who has access to this?" The president managed to open the software and the screen stared back at him dumb.

"Ah, er, this is a security issue?" the Yellow Orang-Utan Industries president stammered.

"Yes," confirmed Naamah Nelise, vice president of the business.

"Have IT been informed? We should probably get one of their security teams on to that, pronto," the president replied with attempted confidence.

"I'll get on to it," Naamah quickly replied and the welcoming sound of a disconnecting phone line arrived in the president's head. He put his phone down. He took in the information on his screen. Gertrude just sat, and watched. She watched the president pale slightly, then pick up the phone again.

"Can I speak to...yes," the president said between nervous finger-tapping. He got through to who he needed to and began chatting. Gertrude stopped watching him and checked her time-piece. She stood and walked towards the president's line of sight. Amongst his mental distraction and yammering he somehow noticed his beautiful assistant. He put his hand over his phone's mouthpiece.

"PR. It wasn't them," he whispered.

"It's time for the meeting. Zabdiel. Accountants. Orange juice." Gertrude countered.

"OK. OK. Thank you...Yes...Thanks, goodbye," the president managed before disconnecting his phone line, the welcome sound of which arrived in a PR employee's head some floors below.

The president rose and buttoned his suit, it was a neat brown. He wore no tie. Gertrude wore black, her jacket featured remarkable shoulder pads. She walked the president to his door and down the hallway. By now it was four minutes past ten.

At twelve minutes past nine that same morning, Pepito was trying to stave off the tiredness claimed from a restless night. The ideas that kept him awake the previous night now had to negotiate their way through the politics of a legal day in the business world. Pepito currently was on the phone to his preferred legal advisor. Their legal discourse was his first challenge to wakefulness he faced in his office today, but he was alert enough to follow its cautionary tone. Eventually the serious part of his legal consultation, questions put to him dutifully answered (phrasing slightly foggy), degraded into final pleasantries and one task for the day came to an end. He quickly moved his attention to updates and enquiries from various teams in his department as well as representatives from other departments in his email inbox. At around ten, he received a relevant update, amid casual follow ups and responses and more thoughts about coffee and Gertrude. It was a security update and it was good news. Wellington was doing very well, a security team was investigating just how well. A quick call through to the team popped to the top of Pepito's to do list. He hit a few buttons on his phone console.

"Hi, it's Pepito here," he said when the call was answered.

"The breach in that Zabdiel Seinfeld program was me. I'm running it through a new analytic computer to improve performance," continued Pepito, he was responded to with some quick questions.

"Any directives the computer adds can be overridden by the users. If things go well, there's upgrade potential for other scheduling applications like these." Pepito paused once again for questions.

"The Zabdiel Seinfeld program was my guinea pig because it has the lowest volume of users, it's separate from the scheduling programs everyone else is logged into around the company. If anything extra the new computer adds to Zabdiel's schedule is dodgy or conflicting with other users' plans, they can be overridden by the users…Yeah. It's OK. You can trust me, you have to, I'm your boss." Pepito laughed, he was getting through, there were less questions to come in this call. His previous call with the lawyers was already realising its usefulness.

"I'm already scheduling a meeting with the users to brief them on the changes with the new analytic computer. So hopefully we can meet really soon and clarify everything. But you can just get back to your inquirers and explain for now that it's part of a software upgrade. That should satisfy them, OK?" Another call of Pepito's degraded into final pleasantries, the call over, he returned his concentration to his office's computer monitor. He still hadn't got a confirmed meeting time with Gertrude though, and that bothered him. He felt he needed to deal with that very soon. Once again it was four minutes past ten.

At sixteen minutes past ten the president of Yellow Orang-Utan had arrived at his scheduled briefing meeting. He had entered quietly, as he was worried about being late, although only there to observe and not having to answer to anyone about attendance. Thankfully the room was darkened as they projected a collection of Telly-net news coverage that mentioned orange juice frequently. The small old man sat amongst members of the board of executive directors, senior accountants, a few senior lawyers and presidential staff. Some of the staff joined the meeting via monitors, including Zabdiel Seinfeld. The monitors had politely been faced toward the briefing presenter, whose Telly-net projection was also fed across the same lines that connected the representatives within the meeting. The less senior accountants were invited to present the meeting to further explain what had been touched upon in the comprehensive report distributed recently. The lighting changed in the room. The Telly-net news coverage was superseded by a graph in the projection.

"This shows share price fluctuation as well as concentration of the orange juice meme over time. And there does appear to be a correlation. We've been looking into how these relate, looking into shareholder demographics and related business that would respond well to some kind of an orange juice PR campaign. Like the sale of 'Dinosaurs 'R' Us', it seems out of character with the aims of our current business direction, but it has been the most well received. These windfalls do come across as anomalous and perhaps for that reason, niggle. Niggle for investigation. How do such flippant or insignificant blips on our business radar wind up with such wide-spreading ramifications and stock market interest. Yellow Orang-Utan Industries has such a vast business portfolio how can anyone, in or out of the company, respective of our PR and marketing, really predict public or shareholder reception of relatively tiny transactions?"

"We're hoping," continued the presenter, "that with our analysis we can understand the so far successful blips like these and capitalise on them. We're also hoping to keep analysing and understand them. Hopefully enough to create these trends a lot better than we do now." Changes in the presentation slides imbued all in attendance with new colours.

"So funding the museum for synthetic entomology could be our next key business move. Selling our ownership of a Sri Lankan popsicle stick factory. Or expanding our line of plastic surgery franchises in Morocco. We're at such early stages in researching this we'd like to try all three, issue a few media releases and see which ones fly." The presenter smiled cheekily, trying not to laugh.

"More importantly, though," he said, "can we tie this to our current aims and direction? Can we unite these anomalies with the overall master plan? With the reception these anomalies are getting, let's hope so." The presenter and several others in attendance exhaled carefully.

"Questions?" offered the presenter. A board member raised a hand and cleared a throat.

"The examples you used as suggested ventures, how serious are they?" The board member asked.

"Well," the presenter began, "the first two remarkable cases seemed erratic and insignificant, yet they trickled amongst major news services enough to reverse the negative coverage we'd been getting about our overall performance, share prices followed suit. Our suggestions here were semi-serious, but are real possibilities, we can only get so much workable data from two cases, and we need some more examples for data and perhaps a reliable model. I hope these examples are sufficiently erratic and insignificant for you." Attendees smiled in response to the answer.

"Well I think you're right about the first two, but not the last one. Not the Morocco one." Heads turned to the sound of the voice. It came from speakers, the ones from Zabdiel Seinfeld's monitor. The president of Yellow Orang-Utan Industries' eyes widened.

"Your analysis is terrific. A little off my page, but very workable, not too far off the page," continued the monitor-sound.

"Ah, thanks," the presenter responded.

"The synthetic entomology idea is timed very well too. I'd already prior to your report arranged an interview with one of their lobbyists. It's in a few days' time." The presenter began to appear a little sheepish.

"What kind of time-frame do you think a working model needs? How long will it take before you think you have sufficient data?" Asked another meeting attendee.

The president looked over at a monitor displaying Letitia Bjorksdottir and then Naamah Nelise. Naamah looked back, eyes as white as the president's and shrugged, raising her hands toward him. The meeting carried on, with Zabdiel Seinfeld leading with some remarkable questions while everybody else continued politely ignoring Zabdiel's involvement in the reasons the meeting was arranged at all. Language referred to the business as a collective 'we' without singling out one responsible person, such as Seinfeld, or the presenter, or the little old man who seemed to be at a lot of important meetings but whose involvement in the business seemed lost somewhere. He looked kind of scared anyway, then relieved when the meeting was finally over. That was at ten fifty-five that morning.

At ten thirty in the morning, Gertrude sat outside the meeting with a small band of personal assistants. Once again she wasn't allowed inside the meeting during these troubled days of Yellow Orang-Utan Industries. She and her fellow barred personnel occupied themselves with their electronic note-makers and pocket computers. It was boring, the décor bland, Gertrude had reclined herself in a chair and began to relax, but got the hiccups. They were quiet hiccups, distracting only to herself, but annoying nonetheless.

Then her phone rang, which Gertrude had temporarily put down when she got the hiccups. She grabbed it and pressed a button.

"Hello?" said Gertrude, then hiccupped. Her phone's caller ID function indicated it was Pepito.

"Hi Gertrude, it's Pepito," confirmed Pepito.

"Oh, hi," Gertrude replied, relieved she knew what this call was about.

"I'm calling about our meeting, have you managed to squeeze it in?" Pepito asked through the phone.

"Ah, yeah," answered Gertrude, "he's in a briefing session with all the presidents and directors at the moment, but that shouldn't be too long. Once we've grabbed some lunch we should be ready for you."

"Can I get a time?" asked Pepito. Gertrude hiccupped again. She glanced at her clipboard while answering.

"Of course, sorry. Er, one fifteen OK for you?" Gertrude suggested.

"That works for me, Gertrude," Pepito answered.

"Do you need me to upload that to your schedule?" Gertrude offered quickly.

"That'd be handy, thank you. Wellington's making waves very quickly. There's already been a security team trying to track his movements with the Zabdiel Seinfeld program that I had to deal with." Pepito was a little relieved to have someone to blab to, Gertrude listened kindly.

"Really? I think I saw the beginning of that. The presidents were talking about it this morning on the phone," she responded.

"Hmm, well, what I'm saying, for now, is the program is undergoing an upgrade. It's being run through a new kind of computer. At one fifteen, I'll start introducing people to the new computer." Pepito said, his tone becoming slightly more stern.

"OK, one fifteen, but for the record, I met the computer first." Thankfully the playfulness of the remark carried across the phone connection. The connected pair both smiled.

"I'll see you this afternoon, Gertrude," finalised Pepito.

"I'm looking forward to it, Pepito. It's exciting," agreed Gertrude, "bye". Gertrude hit a button on the phone and the phone stopped timing the call and became dormant. She wondered what you could eat to cure hiccups and started planning lunch. The time was ten forty.

At eleven O' clock that morning, after Gertrude had ushered the president of Yellow Orang-Utan Industries through hallways and elevators that led to their familiar surroundings of the presidential quarters, the president was back at his desk. He had the Zabdiel Seinfeld scheduling program open and was on the phone to Naamah Nelise, one of two vice presidents at Yellow Orang-Utan Industries.

"Apparently," he said. They were discussing the response they received from their security enquiry earlier that morning. From across the room Gertrude analysed the half of the call audible to her, her own earlier call with Pepito running through her head.

"I assume our director delegates can feed through good or bad reports from the hacking department through the normal channels and we could adjust Seinfeld accordingly," said the little man. He was sounding infuriated despite his life-long rehearsed and businesslike tone. Again, this crease in the running of his organisation required him to do the talking rather than his preferred, but lately perplexing digital proxy.

"By all means," he continued, "get a meeting or a report or whatever you'd like for a clearer picture on this computer." Then the president paused, Gertrude tried to focus on the tinny sound emanating from his phone's ear-piece.

"It's been less than twenty-four hours, Naamah. I'm less worried now, just more frustrated, I can get back to business with Zabdiel Seinfeld's scheduler and it's quite possible the experiment won't make too many waves and eventually blow over. I hope it will." The president wanted all the hassle embodied in the phone call to end.

"This computer has already jumped on the bandwagon cooked up by the young team in accounting," Naamah countered.

"I suppose based on Zabdiel's reaction there'd be no question amongst everyone at the meeting as to whether we'd be green-lighting that proposal," conceded the president.

"The computer's already made that decision for us," added Naamah. Gertrude couldn't quite hear, but did notice the two go on to repeat themselves a few times, perhaps to comfort themselves from the ruffling they'd experienced that morning. Then, buttons pushed and a customary post-call exhalation, and one conversation was over. The president turned on his Wall-span television.

The ensuing news reports feeding through to his enormous monitor were quite glowing. The market was still reacting well to Zabdiel Seinfeld's Yellow Orang-Utan Industries and presenters still made quips about orange juice. The president of the company was reminded of his request to Gertrude for the source of the market tip that had rolled on into his current media consumption. He turned toward her, she was standing in the middle of the room, clutching her familiar clipboard and staring back at him. She wore fetching green shoes, her hair up.

"I have the hiccups," she announced, "shall I order lunch?"

The pair ate their ordered lunch in the usual room. The president had a bread and cheese dish seasoned with novel combinations of herbs and spices while Gertrude had a gluggy risotto with a thick-shake. The president made a typical point of watching her suck on her thick-shake's straw. Gertrude concentrated while swallowing to fight her hiccups, soon she was confident she'd beaten them.

"I've scheduled a meeting for you at one fifteen," she told her lunch companion. The president raised his eyebrows attentively, his mouth full of soft cheese.

"It concerns the source you were asking me for."

"Good. You've found it?" The president had swallowed now and Gertrude's now firm gaze deemed a respectful response.

"Yep." She sipped on her thick-shake. "I think it has something to do with the computer you've been talking about with Naamah this morning, because Pepi from the information technology lab's going to be there."

"Oh, right." The president looked at his array of breads and cheeses and wondered if pieces of puzzle were fitting together.

"Good," he added. "I'm looking forward to it. It could shine a light on a few things, unravel a mystery. Exciting."

"I'm a bit excited too," replied Gertrude, and they both gobbled down on their lunch. When it was finished, the food containers empty, it was nearly one fifteen.

After one fifteen in a meeting room in a magnificent office tower in the heart of the city, Gertrude, Pepito, Wellington and the president gathered. Gertrude was watching Pepito make sure everyone was comfortable and checking if anyone wanted coffee, just as he'd done when he'd introduced her to Wellington the robot. The president of Yellow Orang-Utan happily accepted a coffee order, Gertrude was fine without one, Wellington went along with Pepito and the president.

"I understand there was a security issue this morning with the Zabdiel Seinfeld scheduler," began Pepito.

"Yes. Some kind of computer test. The operators still can override anything the computer tries though," the president confirmed, mid-coffee sip. Pepito exhaled carefully, Gertrude, still observing, guessed he was trying to focus.

"I should confess," began Pepito, "that myself and Wellington here were personally responsible for that upset this morning. You've met Wellington before? He works in market hacking normally."

"I believe you negotiated my contract with me some time ago," offered Wellington. The president sipped his frothy coffee and nodded in agreement, managing a "mmm". Then Pepito continued.

"Wellington has been working with me on the computer test. He's been particularly helpful with his skills in market hacking, the developments he's been making are quite extraordinary. Mostly, because Wellington is the computer we're testing. Wellington is a robot." Pepito looked at Wellington. Everybody looked at the robot. The president stopped sipping coffee.

"I can show you some of my internal mechanics and hydraulics if you find Pepi unconvincing," offered Wellington.

"I suppose," replied the president flatly. Gertrude watched Wellington unbutton his shirt and expose some of his working parts. Her eyes widened.

"Thank you Wellington," said the president and went back to his coffee. "This robot Pepi," he continued, not looking up beyond his insulating paper cup. "This robot is now doing the extra scheduling in the Zabdiel Seinfeld program?"

"Yes," confirmed Pepito.

"Wellington is also the source of the little tips I gave you," piped in Gertrude. The president eyed Wellington carefully, and took another sip on his coffee.

"And now some hot shot team in accounting is trying to predict his next move," he added. "Presumably if that all goes through directions will be sent to market hacking, where Wellington works?"

"Already the team in accounting are proposing ideas that are a bit hit and miss," said Wellington, "if their directions in this form are sent to market hacking, and the hacks aren't followed through or exploited thoroughly, the results won't be as successful. With the increasing downward trend in stock-value and business turnover we've been looking at lately, we can't afford to distract an important department with a collection of weak maybes." Wellington spoke plainly but with a typical earnest confidence.

"Wellington has been increasingly concerned with the future of the company," explained Pepito.

"I'd built him really only to fit in amongst other employees. What has developed is this growing concern for Yellow Orang-Utan as well as some unique insights into market manipulation. I've given due weight to the doubts I've had about the experiment, but no matter how much data I erase from Wellington's memory, it winds up with him insisting on the same ideas, and his results so far have been spotless." Then Pepito took a nervous sip on his coffee.

"Are we suggesting," said the Yellow Orang-Utan president through his coffee breath, "Wellington is a robot who can predict the stock market?"

"I know it sounds incredible," began Pepito, preparing to reply to the president's suggestion. "Wellington, as a machine with some artificial intelligence, wasn't designed to be a computer that can predict the stock market. Even if Wellington was meant to be such a computer, it's not the first computer of its kind. There are plenty of precedents for that, some companies are still toying with them today," he continued.

"Their success has been hit and miss," the president replied quickly. "Yellow Orang-Utan Industries still uses human resources to run its market hacking department. Those computers try to quantify the value of all its information without the intuitions and discriminations of people. It's understanding people that help recognise the butterflies that make up the cyclones."

"Yellow Orang-Utan's market hacking strength is ailing," Wellington chimed in, "it is as hit and miss as the computers you're describing. Excuse me, this is an observation of the present situation." Pepito hadn't quite finished though.

"Wellington has a degree of autonomy that those computers didn't. He has to discriminate like anybody in order to talk socially or even walk through a door. He has limits to his memory, we have to erase sections of it after most of his shifts. Then, it's up to him to reconnect the gaps, like any intuitive, forgetting human. Wellington does this in a way unlike even a very unique organic human, with a human mind. Wellington finds those butterflies.

"Wellington hasn't quite cracked the formula for chaos theory. That's meaning-of-life stuff. But as far as the stock market goes, Wellington can find those butterflies. Chaos theory loves the butterfly effect because it illustrates beautifully those random factors beyond human comprehension, impossible events we can't even begin to imagine. It seems paradoxical that we'll ever find the formula for what exists beyond formula itself. That's kind of the point.

"But the stock market is a human invention, someone imagined it up. All of economics is a human invention, it's, uh, predicated within the parameters of human imagination. It's easily interpreted by hackers and experts, the market is mediated within these parameters.

"So maybe Wellington hasn't sorted out chaos theory for us, but Wellington seems to have figured out the little box humans have slotted economics and the stock market into." Pepito paused.

"Am I explaining this OK? Am I making sense?" The president looked over at Wellington. Gertrude continued to watch Pepito. The president let out a breath that could've been a sigh.

"Go on," he said.

"I mean, even when a random or unexpected event takes place, it falls prey to human value interpretation. Something comes along that we never saw coming, so we go over and over it again in our minds when it does until we've sorted it out. Human media will present something new and surprising over and over again until it's reduced into symbols and something we can trade as a commodity, whether that be cultural or economic. The news of the day, the stuff we watch all the time on Telly-net is an example of how formulaic this phenomenon can be. Surprise announcements, horrible world events are bashed into a retarded collection of tropes and stereotypes limited to relax us like a bedtime picture-book. The first appearance of Yellow Orang-Utan was just such an event and ever since then, Yellow Orang-Utan Industries has made headline news with every move it makes. When everything irrevocably gets trapped within these parameters, is it any wonder Wellington manages to translate the commodities within these limits into formulas for commercial gain?

"I think about it. I think how wrong I could be about this

robot. But this robot has yet to put a foot wrong. Anything he's handled concerning Yellow Orang-Utan or my own stock portfolio has been a success. He finds those butterflies as you put it, he sees those blips on the radar and follows them through, capitalising on their potential with incredible success. At least, he can when he's not trying to keep a low profile in the market hacking department. When he's with me blabbing about how powerless he is to help Yellow Orang-Utan when Zabdiel Seinfeld seems to be overseeing a steady decline, then he seems to be doing his most interesting work." Pepito finally stopped and looked toward the president and then over to Wellington the robot.

"After getting some key tips through with Gertrude and Gertrude's friend Biscoe in PR, with excellent results, Wellington's observations and projections convinced him he would require higher security clearance than a market hacker to do good with Yellow Orang-Utan's future. Wellington then convinced me and I gave him access to the Zabdiel Seinfeld scheduler and requested Gertrude schedule a meeting with you, and here we are." There was nothing left for Pepito to say, he felt naked.

"You'd been asking me for the source of my tips and this works that out for you too, I suppose?" Gertrude added for the president. The president put down his coffee cup.

"This is remarkable news. I suppose I should congratulate you, Pepi, on what an achievement you've made with Wellington."

"Thank you, sir," Wellington replied while Pepito remained quiet.

"Hmm, if this development is to be followed up, other relevant people are going to need to be informed. The vice presidents, the board of directors, the team in accounting that are trying to mimic Wellington as we speak, this should probably be checked with a legal team too."

"The legal check would seem necessary," agreed Pepito.

"But Wellington could mostly operate through Zabdiel Seinfeld anyway. We don't have to let that team in accounting follow through with their plans," Gertrude said thoughtfully.

"No," the president then agreed, "I suppose it might be best to have fewer humans interfering and risking the robot's success."

"It doesn't matter to me," Pepito said, "I've kept Wellington a secret for perhaps too long. I've come clean today and I don't care who else knows. Perhaps consider who you know well enough to trust and go from there. Gertrude's right, Wellington could operate from behind the Zabdiel Seinfeld avatar. Although, I think part of his success is in his normal routine, working in market hacking, lunching with his friends like Biscoe and Gertrude et cetera."

"What exactly are you proposing?" asked the president of Yellow Orang-Utan Industries. Pepito looked at Wellington, then towards the president.

"Taking further steps aren't absolutely necessary at this point. As long as you understand what I've tried to explain today I've got my outcome. Wellington has access to the Zabdiel Seinfeld scheduler, Zabdiel can attend meetings and do business according to Wellington's instructions, provided you don't stop him. As long as that's understood, I'm OK," Pepito replied.

"If Zabdiel Seinfeld is perceived as heading in the right direction, hopefully the rest of Yellow Orang-Utan can follow. Especially in market hacking and PR," added Wellington.

"Alright, thanks very much for this information, Pepi. I guess I should also say it's been nice to finally meet the real you, Wellington."

"It's been a pleasure, sir," replied Wellington in his mathematically likeable tone. The president turned to Gertrude.

"Shall we go?" he asked.

"Yes," Gertrude replied. She turned to address Pepito and Wellington and offered warm farewells, which they returned graciously. She held a door open for the little old man who slowly rose from his chair and wandered through the door frame. The time was one fifty-eight, two minutes to two.

By nine O' clock and sixteen minutes that evening, the president of Yellow Orang-Utan Industries still wasn't sure how he felt about the news presented to him that afternoon. He'd let news feeds on his Telly-net blather for hours and hours, not that kind of news. He'd sent Gertrude home at the usual time and had some dinner ordered up, as well as managing to undress and dress to take a laser shower. As he sat on his enormous bed with silky sheets, backside sagging under the weight of a full belly, he contemplated the source of a numb. He was numb from the shock of this news, the president decided, the robot changed everything. Amidst the evening's winding down of his mind, he resolved to keep an eye on the robot to see what it could really do. As his mind continued to wind down, it began reminding him of his penis, and sex, and he took it upon himself to pick up the phone.

"Yes, sir, what do you want to do this evening?" spoke the familiar voice of Windle through the phone line.

"Windle, good evening, can you transfer me through to an escort agency please?" He asked.

"I suppose so, sir. It has been a while though." Windle said to the request.

"It has, hasn't it?" Agreed the president of Yellow Orang-Utan Industries. At this late hour, it was now seven minutes past eleven.

21.

Today every inhabitant of this planet must contemplate the day when this planet may no longer be habitable.

- John F. Kennedy, 1961

The time was nine hours and fifty-three minutes in the morning. Gertrude had already woken the president and prepared him for the day. She'd scurried off on some errand, or to visit her kiosk or take a call elsewhere, so the president, momentarily, was alone.

It had been some time since the president of Yellow Orang-Utan Industries had learned about the robot Wellington. He'd never come up with adequate reasons to resist his influence over Zabdiel Seinfeld, but neither had he come up with adequate reasons to allow Wellington's influence. Wellington was very quickly accepted as the way things were for the president. The control, the plan he'd had for Zabdiel Seinfeld had become way-laid somewhere, lost amongst theories in accounting and Wellington's computations. Things for Yellow Orang-Utan were slowly improving, the media's coverage was steadily improving and positive. New business ventures were developing to help fill gaps left by retreating investors.

Business continued also for Yellow Orang-Utan's human resources. The departments, their managers, the board of executive directors and the vice presidents were still moving and shaking in their own way. Their projects would gain momentum and make waves, breaking on the news. Those seemed more concrete, the president would feel, and then in typical human fashion, they'd fail somewhere. They'd become linked with scandal, lose legal footing, lose financial interest, momentum would die off. The gap Wellington was slowly filling would slowly widen. But overall, since the president had learned about Wellington, things were not as dire as they had been.

Pepito was allocated a team to assist Wellington. Technicians, accounting experts and market analysts, were monitoring Wellington's progress carefully. Opinion amongst this party in the know, was that to test the limits of this success, to find Wellington's true potential, Wellington needed to be pushed until mistakes and errors were actually made. If the limits could be found, they could gauge how involved Wellington needed to be in running Yellow Orang-Utan Industries' business concerns. Wellington could become like a power plant, turned on when required to fuel the needs of the business, a reservation of market boosting energy.

Organising Zabdiel Seinfeld's daily schedule was a small task that Wellington completed at the end of the day. This was when the links made between the gaps of deleted data in Wellington's memory storage were at their strongest, strengthened by another day of new complimenting data. The accountants and analysts wanted Wellington to schedule more agents within the business programs besides Zabdiel Seinfeld. Pepito agreed this could be done, but hard to test outside of live real time schedulers. In a testing environment, Wellington was no different from the predecessor computers used to predict stock market outcomes. Pepito was also stressing the need for Wellington to have data removed and to go about a normal routine with occasional socialising with friends. These actions seemed instrumental in the way Wellington operated, and Pepito would joke about the robot's work and life balance. Meanwhile Wellington's dumped data was now being stored on other computers for safe keeping, occasionally analysed by others when Wellington made a significant gain. This also meant Wellington could possibly plug back into the data again if useful, so far Wellington usually explained it wasn't useful and concentrated on daily tasks with the normal limited memory capacity.

Slowly though, Wellington worked with other schedulers. At one point everyone in a particular department of Yellow Orang-Utan Industries were assigned tasks that would capitalise on a venture set out by Zabdiel Seinfeld's operations. On another occasion, one of Yellow Orang-Utan's subsidiary companies found themselves getting special attention from Zabdiel Seinfeld, and they also found new tasks they had the option to explore. Once again, Wellington's expanding management of operations was executed in an efficient and trouble free manner with productive outcomes.

Those in the know would discuss each new move and try and be bolder with the next one. Pepito was always erring on the side of caution, nervous of the consequences when or if his robot prototype ventured into wrongdoing and negative return. The greater Wellington's success, the more worried Pepito became. Once, when Wellington had managed to schedule simultaneously multiple branches of Yellow Orang-Utan Industries, the president finally challenged the robot. It was during a meeting where the old man used Zabdiel Seinfeld as his proxy. Seinfeld, with his own pleasant humour, referred to Wellington as his genius new sort-of personal assistant, placing a healthy degree of distance between the artificial pair. But through Zabdiel Seinfeld the president proposed that Wellington be put to the task of scheduling a day of business for the entire corporation, every department, all the subsidiaries.

"Can we do that?" Zabdiel Seinfeld asked the meeting of those in the know. They thought it over and discussed it with Wellington and soon the answer they came to was: "Yes, why not?" Calculations were prepared to determine how much time and logistical orchestrations were needed for the robot to program every scheduler for every human working for Yellow Orang-Utan Industries, for one day.

Today was to be that day. Wellington had planned it over a number of sessions and made it clear that this particular day was the right point to execute their plan. Every single agent operating for Yellow Orang-Utan Industries was under the guiding influence of the robot Wellington. Humans could still ignore their schedules, but never had such a vast number of them had their schedules planned under such a complete vision. Neither had they had such strange but simple requests added there by a robot. Someone was asked to chew gum all day, someone was told what to remark to a call centre operator in an office they had to call, someone was told to sell off shares in a small company, someone had a media release drafted for them, someone else was told to research bison in a particular database at a particular time. For those in the know, all they could do was observe from amongst their own schedules. There was excitement in the air, everybody's routine had been tweaked for the better.

The president of Yellow Orang-Utan Industries, momentarily alone, considered all of this. Today, Zabdiel Seinfeld was off acting as his expertly programmed proxy. He would be paying attention to daily productivity and Telly-net reports. As were a few others in the know, but now it was barely ten O' clock in the morning.

At this time, ten O'clock in the morning, Gertrude wasn't calm enough sitting with the president and wanted to visit and pay her respects to Wellington. Wellington was off duty from the normal market hacker routine and sat with Pepito in Pepito's office helping Pepito navigate progress of the day's business via a glut of live reporting data-feeds. They were cordial greeting Gertrude, but lost for conversation, the suspense of the performance tracking gripped their attention. Occasionally the two would take a call from accountants elsewhere in the building watching the same reports and the parties would consult each other. Gertrude resolved to fetch them coffee, pleased to see Wellington on such a special day. Returning to her superior on the uppermost floor it was more of the same. The president sat glued to the financial news feeds on his Wall-span TV. Eventually, in between messaging Biscuit, Gertrude got to fetch their lunch. After lunch though, Gertrude too became gripped by Yellow Orang-Utan Industries business performance, from about two thirty onwards.

By about three O' clock that afternoon, Wellington's Yellow Orang-Utan experiment was reaching visible fruition. A powerful wave of good business was building up and was visible now from the shores of the market. The news media was still trying to react. The president of Yellow Orang-Utan Industries, sitting on his big bed in a nice suit, looked stunned. Pepito and Wellington, sitting in Pepito's messy office, looked pleased. Gertrude was on the phone to Biscuit to get together for dinner.

The share price was the earliest indicator, the first thing that could be immediately looked upon by Telly-net journalists. But everyone, not just those with little enough to do than watch Telly-net or read other sources of news, was either feeling direct effects of Wellington's work with Yellow Orang-Utan Industries, or aware of what the goings-on were on this particular day. Yellow Orang-Utan Industries was the, or one of the, largest corporations in the world. While people may have had little to do with their core, original line of business, like any giant corporation, Yellow Orang-Utan Industries had, over time, expanded to include a huge portion of other companies' business and product line, as well financial interests in companies that if they didn't own, they virtually controlled.

On this particular day, Wellington, brilliantly or accidentally, though not without careful planning, had tweaked Yellow Orang-Utan's performance within this ubiquity in such a way that these interactions people invariably made with Yellow Orang-Utan Industries left a good impression. The interaction an individual has with the many-tentacled aspects of corporate control could be a genuinely positive one, depending on where emphasis is placed within that interaction. Using that approach on other programs that interacted with people throughout the many infrastructures that collectively made up Yellow Orang-Utan Industries' business on this particular day, meant people were better affected by their computers, and this had further ramifications for the other people and other computers dealing with them, and again others dealing with them and so on and so forth until the movement gained enough force for all to see. Then the value of the share price went up a point, and someone somewhere opted for a Yellow Orang-Utan owned product over another. The business of the day was seemingly profit driven and absurd and pointless as any other company's, yet Wellington had made ventures better, for each agent and recipient in their process. Polite, but idiosyncratic enough to seem genuinely so. This was on such a scale that it was hard to fathom this much personalised pleasantness. Those used to considering the large numbers of corporate business may have the brain power to accommodate it but they were much too distracted by the positive financial returns.

In one fell swoop the conditions were plain to all. The financial world was rocked, news readers wouldn't shut up. Those in the know back at Yellow Orang-Utan Industries were dazzled and shocked. Wellington had broken some kind of record. This was all new. The president was still stunned in a nice suit on a big bed. Wellington and Pepito were still pleased in the messy office. Gertrude was on her way to dinner with Biscuit. Zabdiel Seinfeld was primed for evening news interviews about the surprise of the day's success. It was now five O' clock, the close of business for this particular day.

At seven thirty-two the president of Yellow Orang-Utan Industries walked into *The Swinging Hanky* and took up his booked chair at his booked table. He wasn't entirely sure what had happened to his company today, there was still a numbness in the shock. However, he was sure he needed to be at *The Swinging Hanky* to be out amongst his city's biggest movers and shakers of the business world. Quickly his normal discomfort with socialising took effect and he absorbed himself in the menu. Finding a highly trained attendant nearby, he ordered a cloned bison steak, it had been a popular dish in the restaurant today. It was lost on the president that the business that produced them had recent contact with representatives from Yellow Orang-Utan Industries, which had been the doing of a robot operating a digital avatar and a collection of scheduling programs.

As he enjoyed a pre-dinner glass of wine he noticed the large, chortling figure of Magnum Ndgali amongst the prominent businessmen. Magnum noticed the president too. By the time the president's complimentary bread had arrived at his table, eye contact had been made with nods of acknowledgment.

"Howdy, Arty," spoke Magnum when he eventually came to visit the president's table, halfway into eating his steak.

"Good evening, Magnum. Pleasure to see you," he replied. Magnum stared, pausing and concealing a grin.

"How the hell d'ya do it?" Ndgali exploded. The president smiled back at Magnum's delighted expression.

"I don't even know myself, we had a bunch of young accounting analysts and market hackers, some fancy new program. The details are lost on me. I forget them. Really, I'm as shocked as you are," he replied, and cut deeper into his steak.

"It's really just the work of Zabdiel Seinfeld now," he added.

"You were going down, Arty. Way down. But this? You're top dog again, bigger than before now. Without me! Without me and you're still bigger." Magnum seemed close to laughter.

"You want back in Magnum?" asked the president, "I can't verify how long we can sustain this level of success." He grinned while concealing the food he chewed.

"Of course! I want my piece of this. I'll be buying whatever my guys can get their hands on that's affiliated with you now. You coy bastard. I should have held on back when you told me to," exclaimed Magnum, punching the table.

"We're all a bit shocked today, Magnum. I wasn't sure about Zabdiel Seinfeld then either. After this, well, I'm not sure about him now either."

"Cautious, Arty. Always, cautious. I gotta take everything you say with a grain of salt. I'll be back in soon, you betcha." Magnum was hailed over at another table and he bid the president of Yellow Orang-Utan Industries a friendly farewell. The president set about finishing his steak. This was followed by a wobbly custard pudding. During the pudding the president received a message, signalling a later appointment. It was time for him to finish up and get going. That time happened to be eight twenty-one in the evening.

At about ten minutes to eight earlier that evening, Gertrude and Biscuit were hugging. They'd now both arrived at their selected restaurant for their evening's dining. The restaurant was called *Cowhorn* and all the furniture there was made of cane, the décor too of various woven plants. Telly-net monitors mounted from the ceiling there were espousing the wonders of Yellow Orang-Utan Industries, and they'd been witness to why.

"Sorry I'm late," Gertrude said first.

"Forget about it, pull up a chair," replied Biscuit, and they wrangled themselves some wicker chairs and sat down.

"Wellington's phone's been off, all day," said Gertrude, "but I did pop in to see him today. I brought him and Pepi a coffee."

"I'm so proud of him," added Biscuit with a grin. They grinned together, before distracting themselves with their surroundings.

"This place looks great, very summer-y," remarked Gertrude.

Biscuit ordered them each fuzzy navels in tall glasses, her latest drink of choice. They ordered food, but it had a hard time competing for attention with the still unfolding news.

"Do you think they'll make Wellington president?" asked Biscuit.

"He's kind of operating as president now. Today he probably had more influence over the whole company than any president ever had," answered Gertrude.

"It's pretty amazing," Biscuit exclaimed.

"Yep," Gertrude agreed. They returned to their food. Biscuit paused, still thinking about what Gertrude already understood.

"Wow, the whole company, that's huge, He controlled the whole thing today, it's very, um..."

"Manipulative?" Gertrude suggested.

"I suppose so, yes, manipulative." Biscuit concluded, before eating again, and thinking again.

"He would make a fine president though, wouldn't he? I'd like to see him on the news all the time. He's more like a Piano Smedley than Zabdiel Seinfeld will ever be," Gertrude said, before Biscuit could start again. The two laughed and grinned amidst nods.

"Do you think our friendship with him helped make him such a successful robot?" Biscuit eventually got out. This made Gertrude think.

"I guess so, yes. I mean, he gets information from us when we chat and that contributes, doesn't it? I wonder? He used us being friends to relay information to my boss and that started things rolling for him. Goodness." Gertrude paused, her breathing had slightly quickened.

"We met when Piano Smedley died, didn't we?" Gertrude asked. Biscuit nodded in agreement while swallowing some stir-fry.

"Do you think both meeting Wellington later on helped keep us together as friends? Having Wellington in common?" Gertrude asked. Biscuit thought for a moment, staring at her dish heightened by synthesised colours.

"Mutual friends help people stick together, of course!" replied Biscuit.

"To us, then" Gertrude declared, and raised what was left of her drink to toast. Biscuit toasted back and their smiles widened to grins.

"If Wellington does become president, I'm not sure he'd have as much time for us," declared Gertrude.

"I'm grateful for any of the time I've spent with him at all," Biscuit replied, "he always makes me feel great when I was around him. He was always friendly and cordial and I loved every minute of it." Gertrude still looked a little thoughtful.

"I'm still thinking about how knowing us meant he could relay information to my boss. So much of making us feel great interacting with him allowed him to get his own way, without any of us feeling like he had an agenda. But he sort of did, he was a robot with programming and directions from Pepi, although Pepi seemed surprised by Wellington sometimes too. I wonder how calculated that was and I feel a little uncomfortable, like when we found out Piano wasn't real or when he died or something.

"But you're right Biscoe. He was so nice to us, a friend amongst that too. And we're better friends for knowing him. I could think through every little interaction we had with him. I could try and figure out how every detail discussed he used to advance his career or something. But that's all offset by how genuinely we appreciated his company. He was a positive influence. He made our lives better and you're right Biscoe, we need to appreciate that."

"Gertrude, I think you're being too existential," Biscuit responded.

"You're right, I'm sorry, you're so right," agreed Gertrude, "I need another drink." Biscuit furrowed her brow quickly.

"Was existential the right word?" she asked earnestly. Gertrude laughed. Their next drinks arrived at eight forty-two that evening.

"No?" asked an escort at eleven seventeen that night.

"No" agreed the president of Yellow Orang-Utan Industries, and the escort removed their attention from the president's genitals. The Telly-net porn they'd accessed earlier played on. The escort resumed caressing broader regions of the old man's withered form. The Telly-net pornographers screamed with delight. The president sighed, he was trying, this was effort.

"It's been such a long time," he complained.

"Since -?" began the escort.

"- Since I had an erection," the president interrupted.

"Take a pill. Take a pill and you could do me all night long," suggested the escort.

"I'm usually allergic to pills, or implants, or any of that cosmetic stuff. Look at my eyes." The president explained, and so the escort moved closer to his face.

"I've been blind a bunch of times and I have eye replacement operations, not with synthetics or clone eyes, but old fashioned all organic donor eyes."

"Uh, huh," remarked the escort, "you can't get an all organic penis donor?"

"There's more to it than that, isn't there? It could be my brain. Brain replacements have different results," the president replied. Then he rolled over.

"The last person I had sex with was my personal assistant," he confessed with a sigh.

"Why don't you do it again?" asked the escort.

"That was ages ago, before I had any problem. And I guess it wouldn't be the same now. We've both changed now. She seems more focussed and professional, and less emotional." The Yellow Orang-Utan president paused. The two could hear each other breathe.

"I couldn't do it with her now. Even if I got my own problem sorted out, I couldn't do that with her again," he added. There was another pause, which was a little too intimate for the escort with the old man, as much as she was enjoying the enormous bed.

"Are you sure?" she asked.

"Yes," he confirmed, a lump in his throat audible.

"Besides, I think I'm going to fire her." The time was eleven thirty.

22.

You know, I could probably cut him down, but there's this odd look of mayhem on his upside down face.

- Lake Placid, 1999

At the exact time of eight forty-five in the morning the door to the Yellow Orang-Utan Industries information technology laboratory opened, allowing Pepito access to his workplace. He wended his way through corridors and common rooms until he reached the door to his office. He would normally use a security card to gain access to his office but today the door was open. Furthermore, his normally cluttered office was looking rather bare. Two men were already busy in his office boxing its contents.

"Hello?" Pepito called to the strangers. The two men in suits turned to greet the call.

"Pepito?" asked one man.

"Pepi, yes," confirmed Pepito.

"Hi, we're from security," the speaker explained. Pepito knew a lot of security teams, Yellow Orang-Utan Industries security teams often worked through these issues from offices in the information technology laboratory. These two men were not of that ilk. This was something Pepito wasn't used to and uncomfortable with.

"What's going on?" he asked, a little desperate.

"Your work has been reclassified and we have to move it to a higher security area." One of the security men explained.

"Oh," reacted Pepito.

"We'll need to ask you a few questions too. Do you mind waiting? Otherwise I may be required to restrain you." The security man had a friendly manner, this was executive security.

"Uh, where's Wellington?" Pepito asked quickly.

"The robot-man? He's already locked up and under investigation. Our department got orders for this really late last night."

"Investigation?" blurted Pepito.

"We're nearly finished here," offered one security guard.

"Are you ready?" the other guard asked Pepito. Archive boxes and Pepito's computer equipment were now loaded on a trolley. He watched one man wheel it through his office door and he sheepishly began following it, flanked by the second security guard. Pepito was quite confused now.

"Am I being sacked or something?" he asked.

"We don't really know, buddy. Someone else has the full briefing back at our office. You'll probably get the complete run-down when we get there," one replied.

The three continued their laden-trolley progress through corridors and common rooms while Pepito ran rapid-fire scenarios through his head. He already knew the robot's personal phone was in the archive boxes in front of him, and from what he'd been told so far, the room where Wellington would recharge, have his tummy-bag emptied and his memory erased or backed up was already packed up like his own office. Inside Pepito's hot brain, he allowed himself a sigh that became a whimper. The time was nine O' clock in the morning.

At five minutes prior to nine O' clock in the morning, Gertrude had woken the president. Telly-net porn was still playing on the Wall-span TV when she got there. She'd turned it off before waking him. The president mumbled something about coffee and Gertrude organised to have some brought to him, a cup for her too. She helped the old man get dressed. He'd turned the Wall-span back on to watch more Yellow Orang-Utan news via Telly-net. Gertrude organised breakfast, they ate quietly. The president was saying very little, stony.

They returned to where the president kept his desk and his gigantic television screen. The news played on, still reeling from Wellington's executed calculations. Gertrude, rapidly bored, wondered if Wellington would be contact-able today. Gertrude, instead, got an enigmatic message from Pepito. She read it on her phone while the president stared at his desk computer, idly clicking on a mouse.

"Do you know what's happening to Pepito?" Gertrude asked, snapping the president out of his funk. He looked up at her still clutching her lit up phone.

"Mmm?" he enquired.

"Pepi, head guy at the info tech lab? He built Wellington?" continued Gertrude.

"Well, you're aware how much of Wellington's work went into the events that happened yesterday? I mean, it's on the news right now isn't it?"

"Yes," answered Gertrude quickly, Pepito had informed her that he might be getting fired and wanted to know if she was OK.

"The scale of operation that Wellington's working from is incredible. The level of detail in everything Wellington can manipulate is amazing. I must admit that Wellington, what he can do, it makes me uncomfortable," said the president. Pepito's message was making Gertrude uncomfortable now, it also relayed that Pepito had lost contact with Wellington too.

"Wellington's powers of manipulation make me nervous. When I check his employment records to find just how long Wellington's been operating at Yellow Orang-Utan, they go back awhile. Wellington won't be involved with Zabdiel Seinfeld and higher end decision making for a while. Wellington's under investigation until we can clear up exactly what his past work history has been."

"What exactly do you think you'll find? All this robot goes on about is helping the company." Gertrude enquired.

"Specifically, Gertrude, I want to know how involved this robot was with the death of Piano Smedley. Nobody really planned for Piano to die, it seemed random and out of the blue. But that's exactly where Wellington's ideas seem to come from. If this robot sincerely believes it's this company's saviour, how many of Yellow Orang-Utan's presidents will be de-railed in order for Wellington to save it?" Gertrude's mouth opened.

"And Pepi? Gertrude probed. The president leaned back a little in his chair.

"Hmm, well, Pepi made Wellington. We've separated them and Pepi's getting questioned too. He's seen more than anybody else what Wellington's been up to. We have to check if their stories line up. Pepi has, of course, been involved with as much of building Piano Smedley and Zabdiel Seinfeld as he has with Wellington, it seems unlikely he'd purposefully design one to destroy the other."

"I suppose," agreed Gertrude.

"I think, for me personally, my discomfort with Wellington, this is the stepping off point for me. I'm getting too old for this game. The investigation is, I guess, some kind of formality before Wellington gets given the reigns for good. From the business point of view it makes sense, I have to concede that. But my distrust of the robot, well, I don't want to be any part of that. I'll step aside, but only so far, to still permit me a few protests before I go. I made this company and I can't give up easily, I've gripped on most of my life. So I guess the investigation is one of these protests. No doubt Wellington will talk a way out of it." The president had risen from his chair, fidgety. He straightened, turned and faced the window, looking out on a city blessed to host the headquarters of the most successful of corporations ever.

"I'm going to retire, Gertrude. I'm going to move into one of those island getaway properties I've got stuffed away in my real estate portfolio, and hopefully never come back. Not without one or two more of these formal protests. It's my right as perhaps the last real human president of Yellow Orang-Utan Industries."

"Which means, I think, I may have to let you go," admitted the perhaps last real human president of Yellow Orang-Utan Industries. "We could reassign you as PA to someone else at Yellow Orang-Utan, of course," he offered.

"No," Gertrude answered quickly, if she was to be let go, she knew she wanted a clean break. The president looked at her, surprised.

"I should be able to look after myself," she explained.

"Oh? Good for you, I'm glad to hear it. I guess I'll jet off in a couple of days. Gertrude, thank you. Thank you for your years of excellent service, we'll have Zabdiel Seinfeld whip you up an excellent reference, of course," replied the president.

"Thank you," Gertrude responded. The president turned back to the window.

"You have to know when to stop, Gertrude. When it's time to say 'no more'. My time has come. Finally I'm getting off the Yellow Orang-Utan train." The president followed that with a tired sounding sigh.

"That's it?" asked Gertrude.

"That's it," confirmed the president, "let's finish off the day, shall we? I need you to book me an appointment with Dr. Westaway, whenever it's convenient for him." The president sat back down at his desk, a little shy about facing Gertrude.

"What shall I say it's about?" asked Gertrude, picking up her clipboard. The president inhaled carefully.

"Well, I'm impotent," he admitted. The time was ten O' clock and forty-five minutes.

As soon as she had the chance, around twelve minutes past eleven, Gertrude contacted her friends to share her news. She let Pepito know she was OK. She agreed to meet Sensae and Prudence for drinks after work. She spoke to Biscuit too, who called in response to the news.

"Yes, I'm going to be OK," Gertrude assured her, "it is a big deal and I think I'm still numb, but it's a good kind of numb. I'm excited." Biscuit asked about Wellington.

"Well, they've taken him somewhere, Pepi too. I was told they're under investigation. I've also been told that they might let Wellington be president eventually though. It may take a while." Gertrude's phone earpiece vibrated slightly in reaction to Biscuit's response.

"No, we still can't get him on the phone. Pepi can't get him either. He's under investigation, presumably some security team or a legal team have him somewhere. Biscoe? Biscoe, it's gonna be OK. Do you want to meet me for a drink at *Fishpaste* tonight?" The vibrations slowly eased. The time had become half past eleven.

At two minutes past three that afternoon, the president of Yellow Orang-Utan Industries had let Gertrude, his personal assistant, go home early. She'd booked his appointment with Dr. Westaway for tomorrow, so he was left to call his real estate agent and get himself moved into a new residence. Presumably his island mansion would already be fully furnished and filled with the modern conveniences in infotainment media. The phone call was made, the president turned next to his computer to book a flight to the island he'd just discussed. Yellow Orang-Utan Industries had a few jets of their own. With that done he returned to staring at the Zabdiel Seinfeld scheduling software. There was one final surprise waiting for him to reveal to everybody, one more little protest and then he'd walk away. Zabdiel Seinfeld had a very busy schedule since Wellington started creating more business for him and Yellow Orang-Utan. But the president could override any of it he wanted, so he made time for Zabdiel Seinfeld to make a special announcement. By three thirty he was done, and so he ordered up a drink.

So, at six thirty that evening Zabdiel Seinfeld appeared on a prominent Telly-net site and made an announcement, and the news of that carried forth. The retiring president watched it from his big bed with a celebratory drink in his hand. Gertrude noticed it on screens throughout the city as she made her way to Fishpaste where undoubtedly it would keep on playing. It played on Biscuit's lounge-room television while she lay curled on her couch having a cry before she got up to take a shower. Wellington and Pepito may have seen the announcement, but no one could contact them to confirm this.

Zabdiel Seinfeld announced that he too was stepping down as president of Yellow Orang-Utan Industries, and considering retirement. Furthermore, the presidency was to be assumed by a long-term Yellow Orang-Utan employee who was currently in cryogenic suspension. Zabdiel Seinfeld would not reveal the name of the employee, citing their request not to have their cryogenic suspension made known to their family. After the boom in activity at Yellow Orang-Utan Industries just prior to his announcement, Zabdiel Seinfeld acknowledged his vice presidents and board of executive directors, stockholders, particularly new stakeholders who were new to Yellow Orang-Utan and other levels' managers and decision makers at the company, then thanked them wholeheartedly. Zabdiel Seinfeld said it was their great success that helped prompt his decision, that credit was entirely due to them. He could not comfortably accept any responsibility, even as president of the corporation and his stepping down was in fact a gesture of faith and kudos to his company for their amazing work. By no means did he mention the robot who'd orchestrated the multi-faceted campaign that led to the unprecedented success, nor its creator, nor the possibility that there may be a link between this success and the death of Piano Smedley.

Meanwhile the other retiring president of Yellow Orang-Utan Industries raised his glass towards his Wall-span TV, in victory. He was old, he was moving to his island getaway, but he would probably die there. He owned a controlling share of Yellow Orang-Utan stock which he could, when he died, bequeath to Si'ng in cryogenic suspension. Presumably because he would die before Si'ng came out of cryogenic suspension. This would only add to Si'ng's power as the legally active president of Yellow Orang-Utan Industries. This was what the news reporters were commenting on now and for the rest of the evening, the legal difficulties concerning people in cryogenic suspension. The corporation with a strong legal team would find workable means around this, of course, the old man knew that. Zabdiel Seinfeld still had a few Telly-net appearances scheduled for this evening, they were to be about some of the exciting new business happening at Yellow Orang-Utan Industries from Wellington's campaign. Obviously now there would be some extra questions about his stepping down and the newly appointed president, this the digital avatar would handle with the pleasant diplomacy allowed him by conversational software. That was later, for now the time was ten minutes to seven in the evening.

At twenty-six minutes past six earlier, but only just, that evening, Biscuit was curled up on her couch and she began crying. Her friend Gertrude had lost her job at the corporation where they worked and wanted her to come out to her favourite bar and party. Not having her around at work to talk to anymore was upsetting. So, she was crying. Zabdiel Seinfeld, the president of the corporation they worked for, appeared on her Telly-net monitor to make an announcement. She didn't notice. Between the sobs she had another distraction, from her handbag on the floor came the familiar call of her phone, a distraction she needed.

"Hello?" she said to the device, while Zabdiel Seinfeld mumbled on.

"Hallo Biscoe, it's Wellington," was the response that came through the connecting line. After the phone call Biscuit leapt from the couch, her eyes quickly drying. She had a new secret, and she needed now to shower and go celebrate with Gertrude. The time was now ten minutes to seven.

At about five minutes past seven, Gertrude sat alone at *Fishpaste*, waiting for her friends to arrive. She'd arrived early as earlier that day she'd been permanently released from service as the personal assistant to the president of Yellow Orang-Utan Industries. Prudence and Sensae arrived at the media-bar.

"Hooray," cried Gertrude as they appeared, throwing her arms in the air. She greeted them more formally when they reached her booth. They asked of her job and she smiled, laughed, repeatedly used the term "freedom" and raised her glass to them. By the time her friends' respective latest lovers had arrived the agenda for the evening was clear. Gertrude had talked to Sensae about some pills, specifically "happy" ones which once supplied, she popped with glee. The others were encouraged to drink, and they did, if only to catch up with her. She'd be dragging accomplices to the dance floor, when it was Prudence she'd discuss the available gentlemen she spied in the bar. Thankfully her enthusiasm was genuine and contagious. Strangers in the bar became ensnared in her revelry too.

Biscuit arrived in time for Gertrude to still be sober enough to notice. Very soon the two one-time colleagues were dancing with abandon on the dance floor, illuminated by Telly-net screens playing stories of the day. Many of the screens were, justifiably, running content concerned with Yellow Orang-Utan's business dealings as well as Zabdiel Seinfeld's announcement earlier that evening. With enough drinking and dancing, Gertrude reduced the many screens to irrelevant blurs.

The evening ended when Gertrude found a bartender whose shift was over and she scurried off home with him, intent on screwing him into exhaustion in the spirit of celebration. Her friends soon realised she was gone, and after a phone message to Prudence, they understood what was going on. They finished their drinks and offered each other their farewell. Gertrude's night was finally over at about four or five in the morning, she didn't check the time.

About the author:

Simon Gray started writing *Yellow Orang-Utan Industries* in about 1997.
He contributed to & published small press zines & comics since 2000 &
hasn't stopped.
In 2004 he earned a rare condemnation from the Flinders University
Student Council for publishing his strip, *Simon The Evil Bastard* while
editing their Student Association's publication *Empire Times*.
He was mired with Adelaide's Format artist collective, usually for zine
related or entirely strange projects, from 2008 to the demise of their Peel
Street premises, 2013?
In 2012, he anthologised his 2006 zine series for print on demand:

lulu.com/shop/simon-gray/simon-gray-2006/

He lives in a sharehouse near the Adelaide Airport, with no children, no
pets, & half the furniture constructed from milkcrates.
On the internet he's often buried under articles about a dead UK
playwright, these links are more specific:

redbubble.com/people/yummylychees
etsy.com/shop/distractomat
twitter.com/yummylychees
yummy-lychees.livejournal.com/